Children of Other Lands

Coloring Book

Vintage illustrations were first published in 1938

Republished by Mountainview Press ©2017

Thank you for purchasing this book. May you find this collection useful in learning about traditional dress of children in many countries around the world. People often express their identity through costume. It is usually associated with the country they are from or, the time they lived in history. If the costume is used to represent a specific ethnic group, it is known as traditional clothing. Most of the clothing in this vintage coloring book are traditional dress that children living in countries around the world wore at special celebrations. Each child in the illustrations are given a name common to that culture. Today people still like to express themselves through clothing, especially at special events or celebrations.

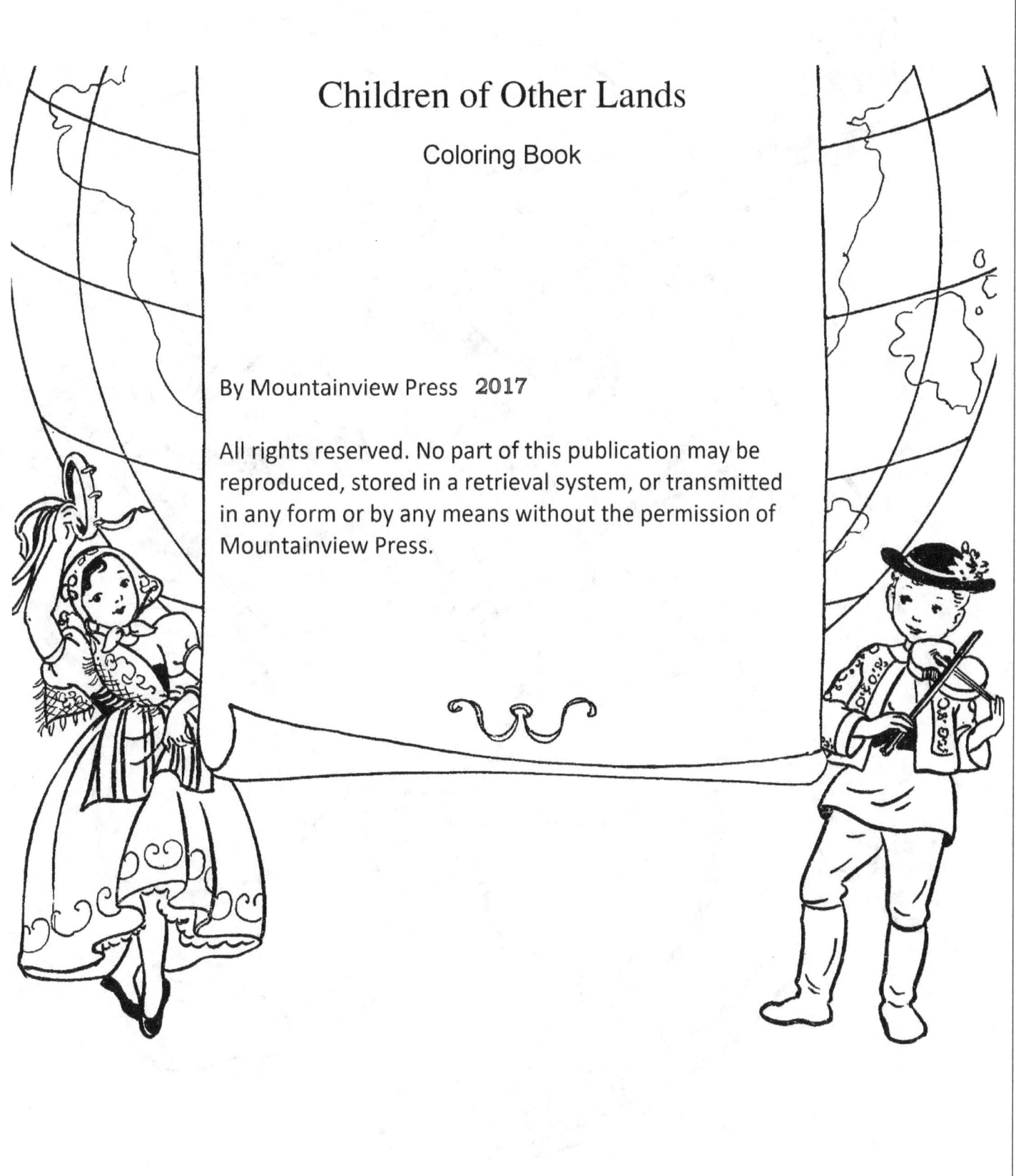

Children of Other Lands

Coloring Book

By Mountainview Press 2017

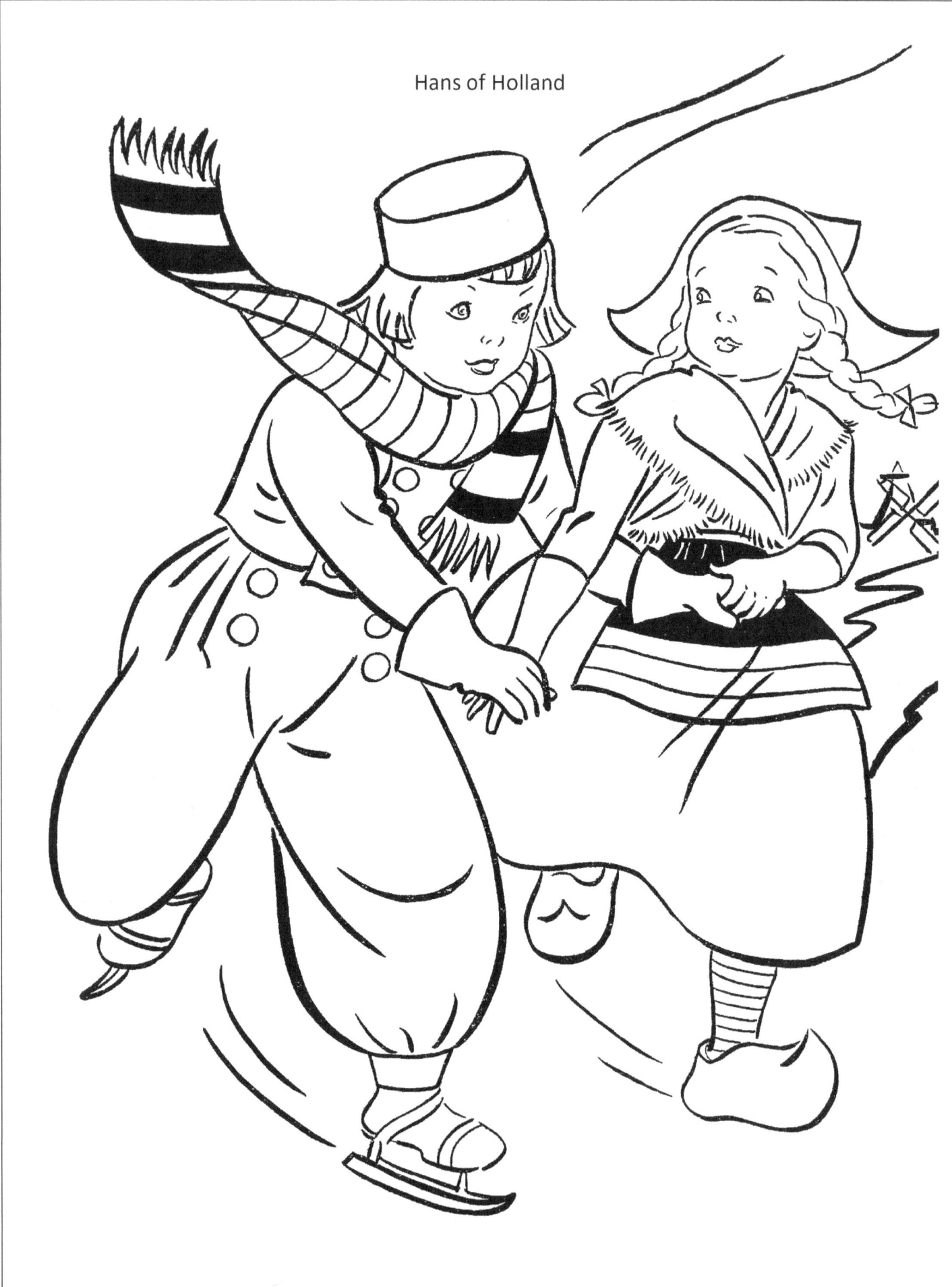

Gretchen of Holland

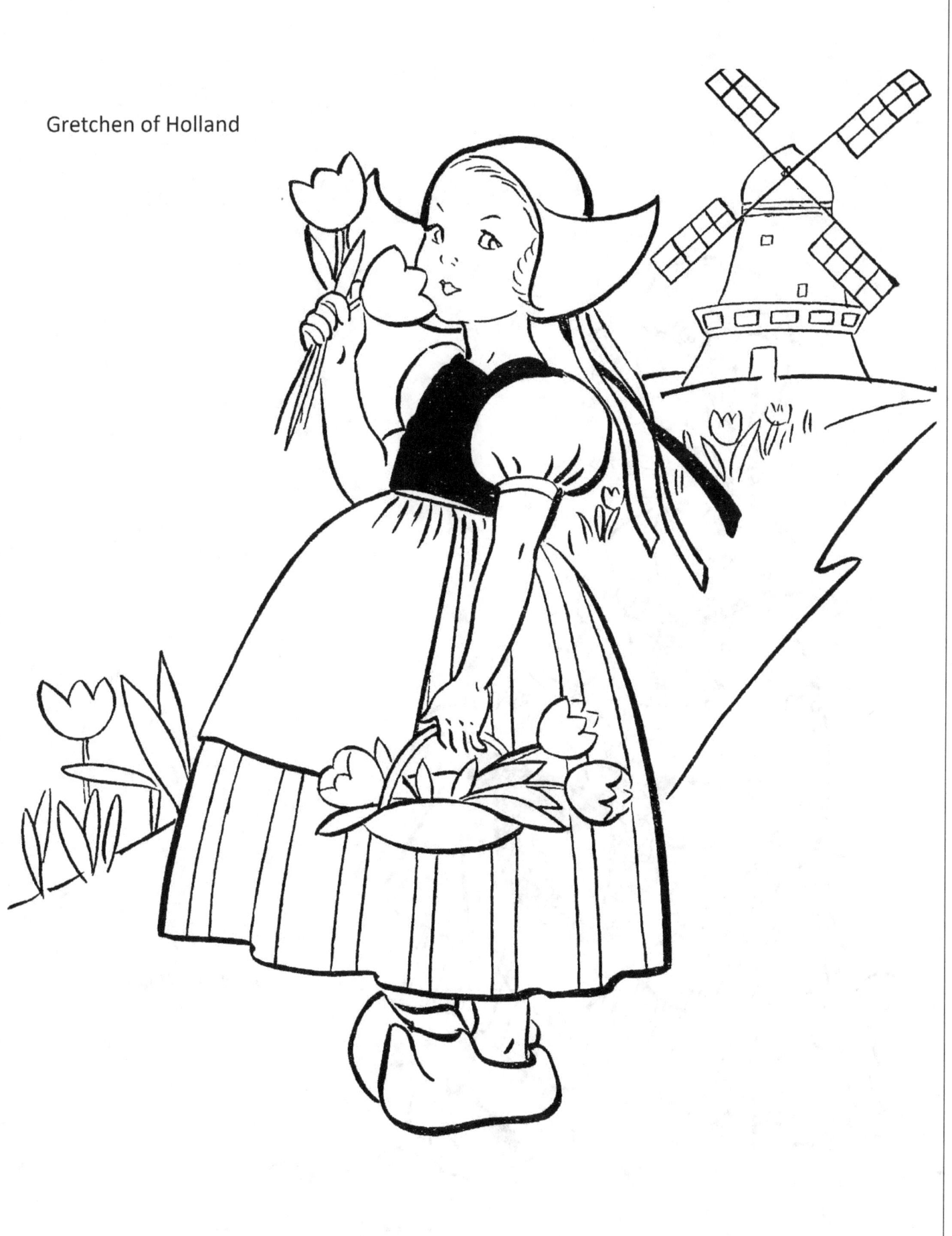

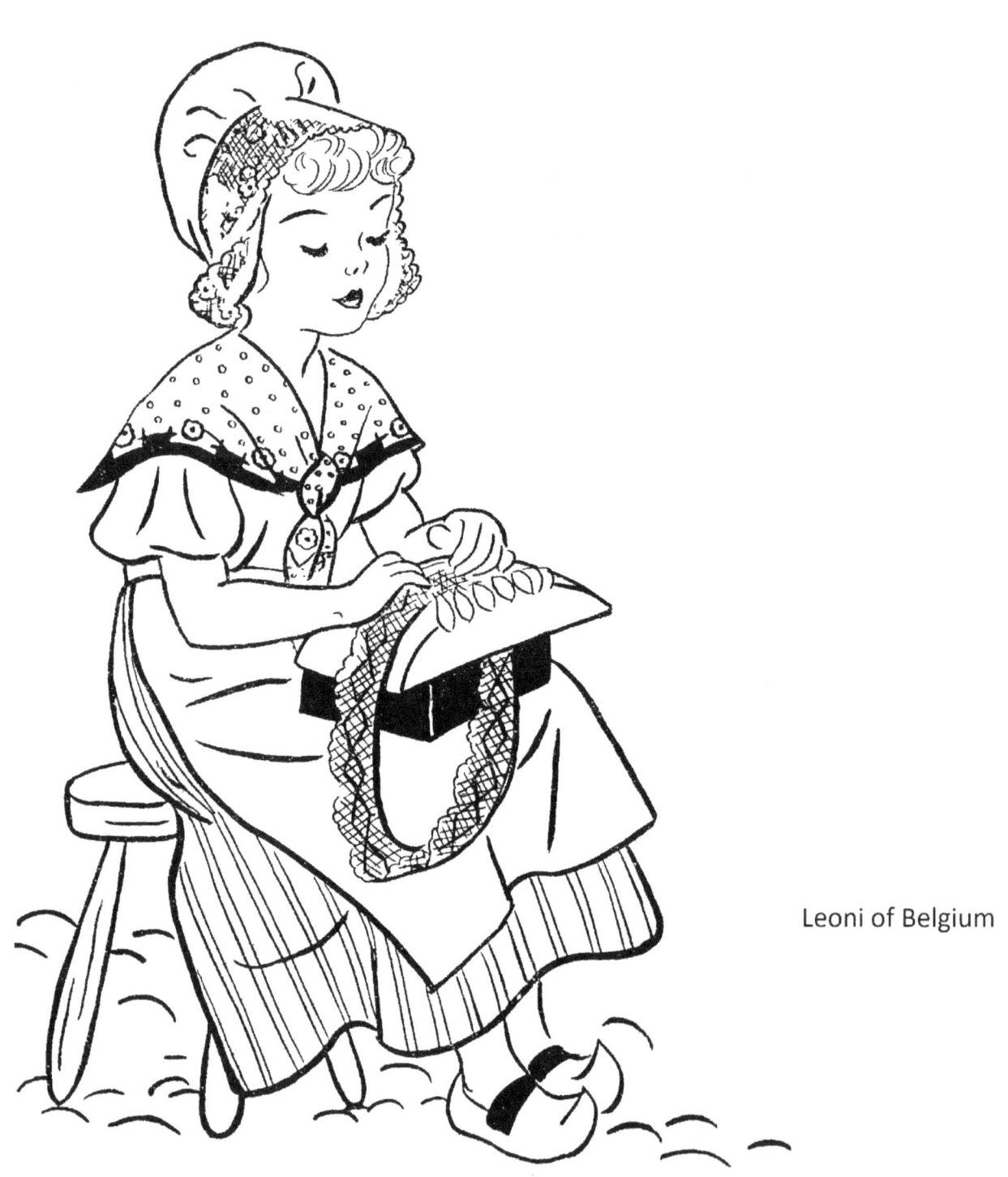

Leoni of Belgium

Anita of Norway

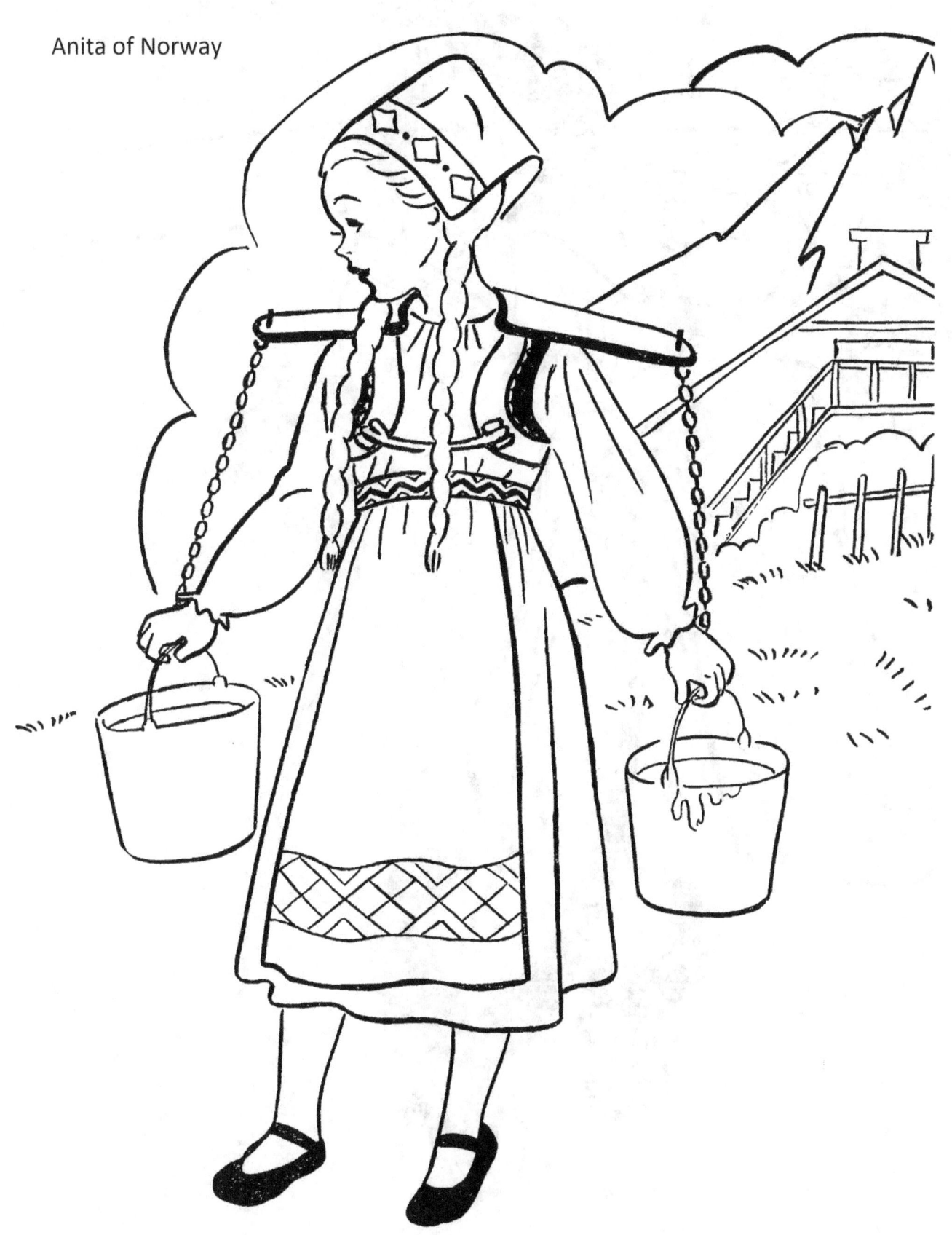

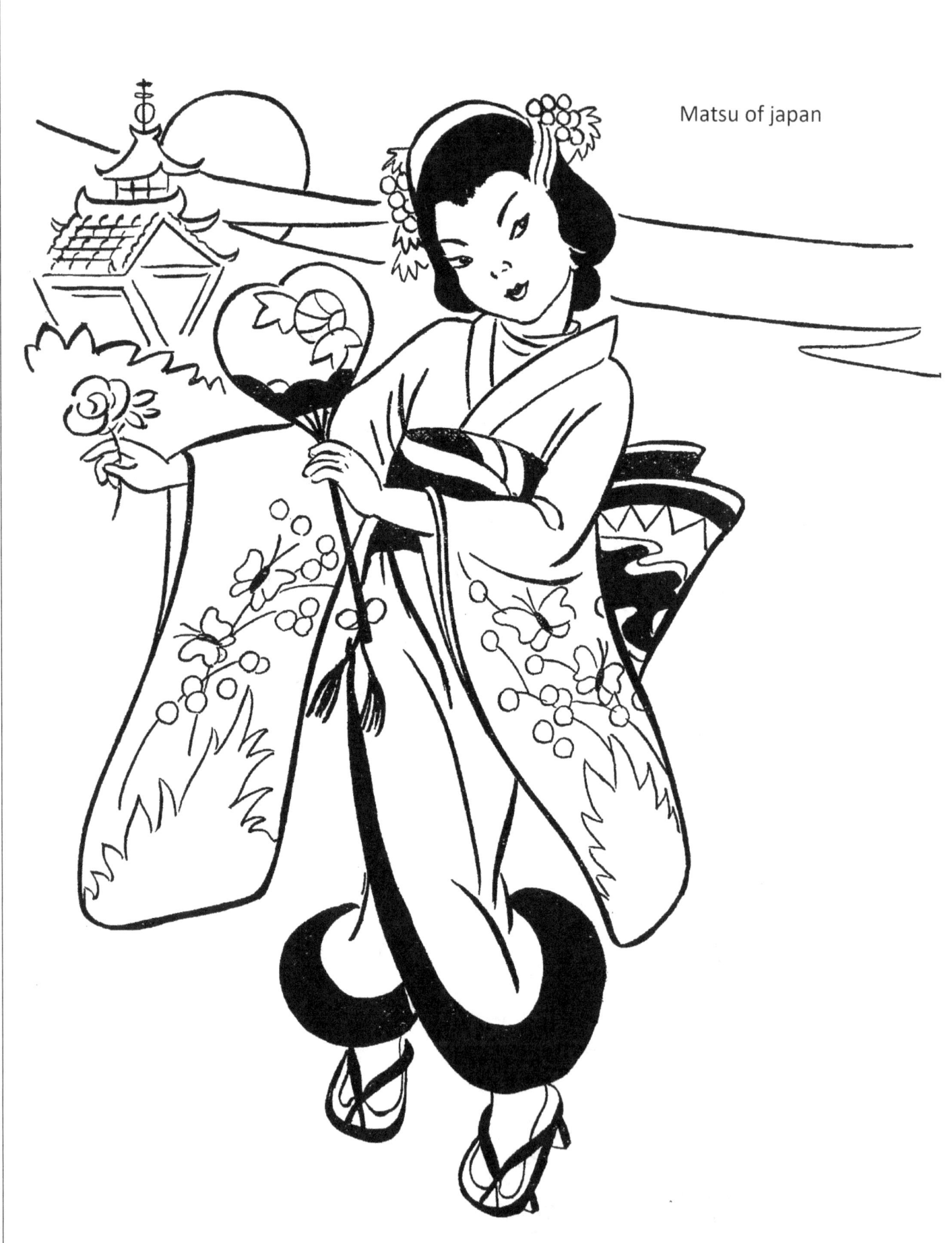

Matsu of japan

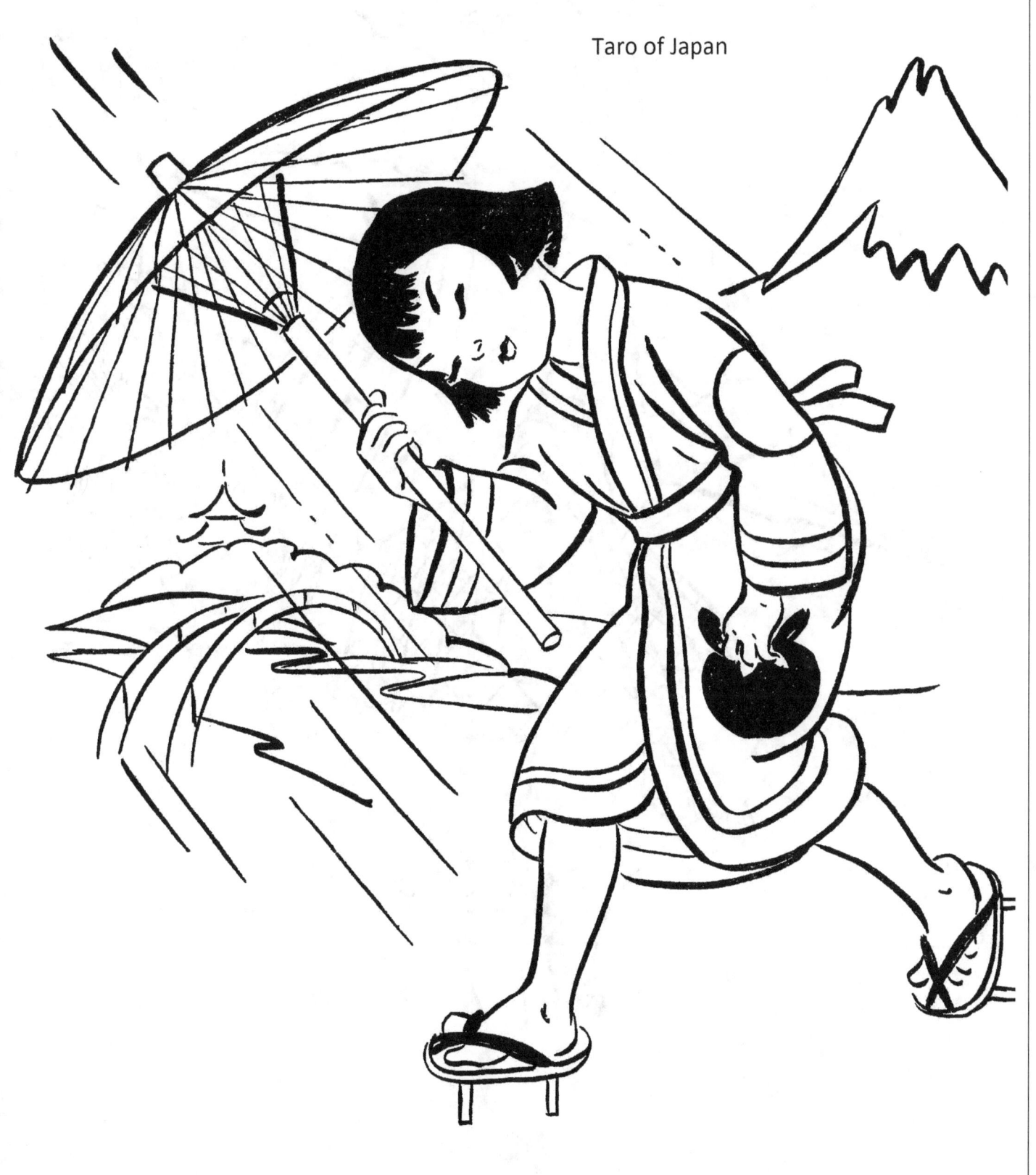

Taro of Japan

Douglas of Scotland

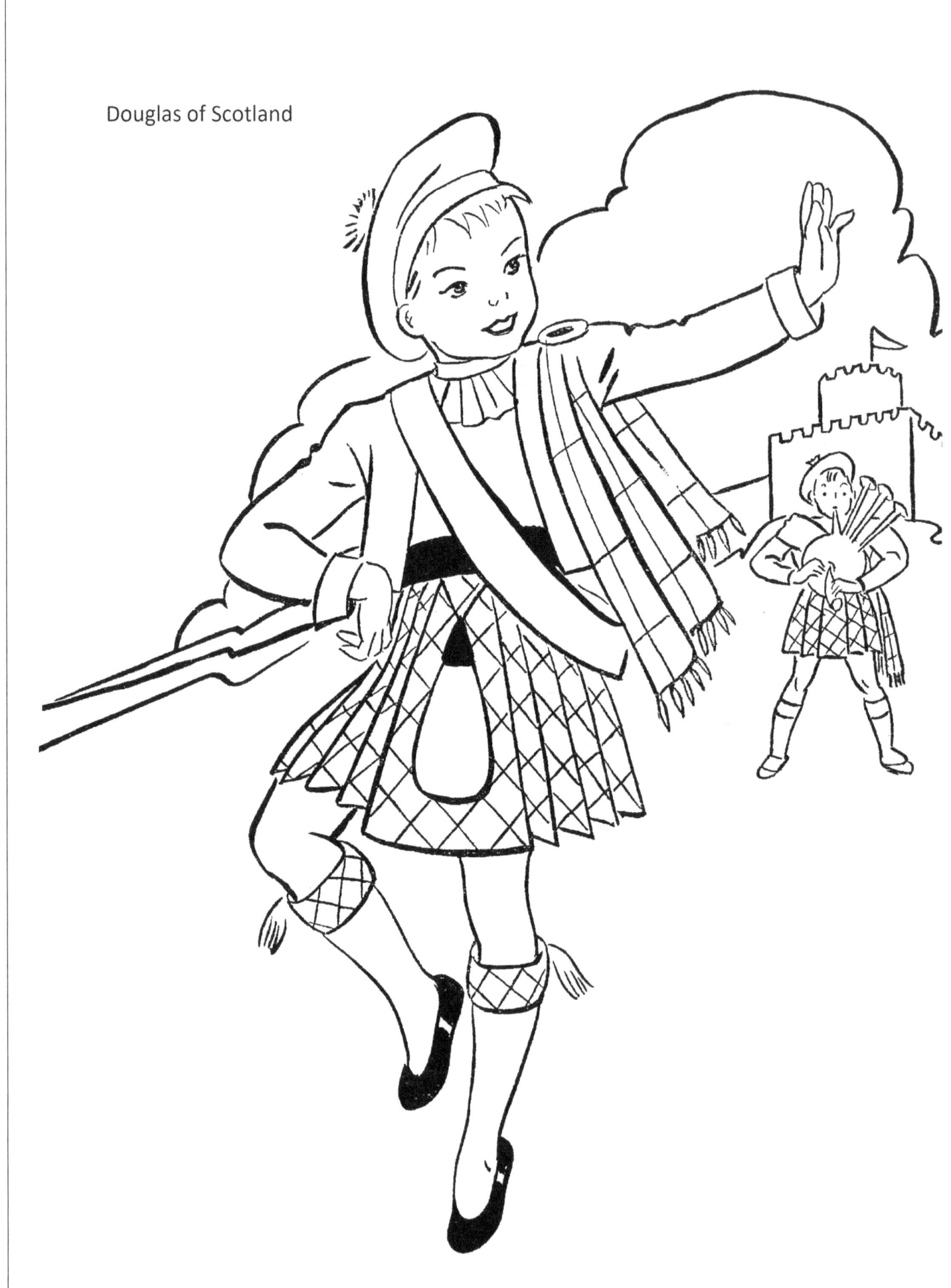

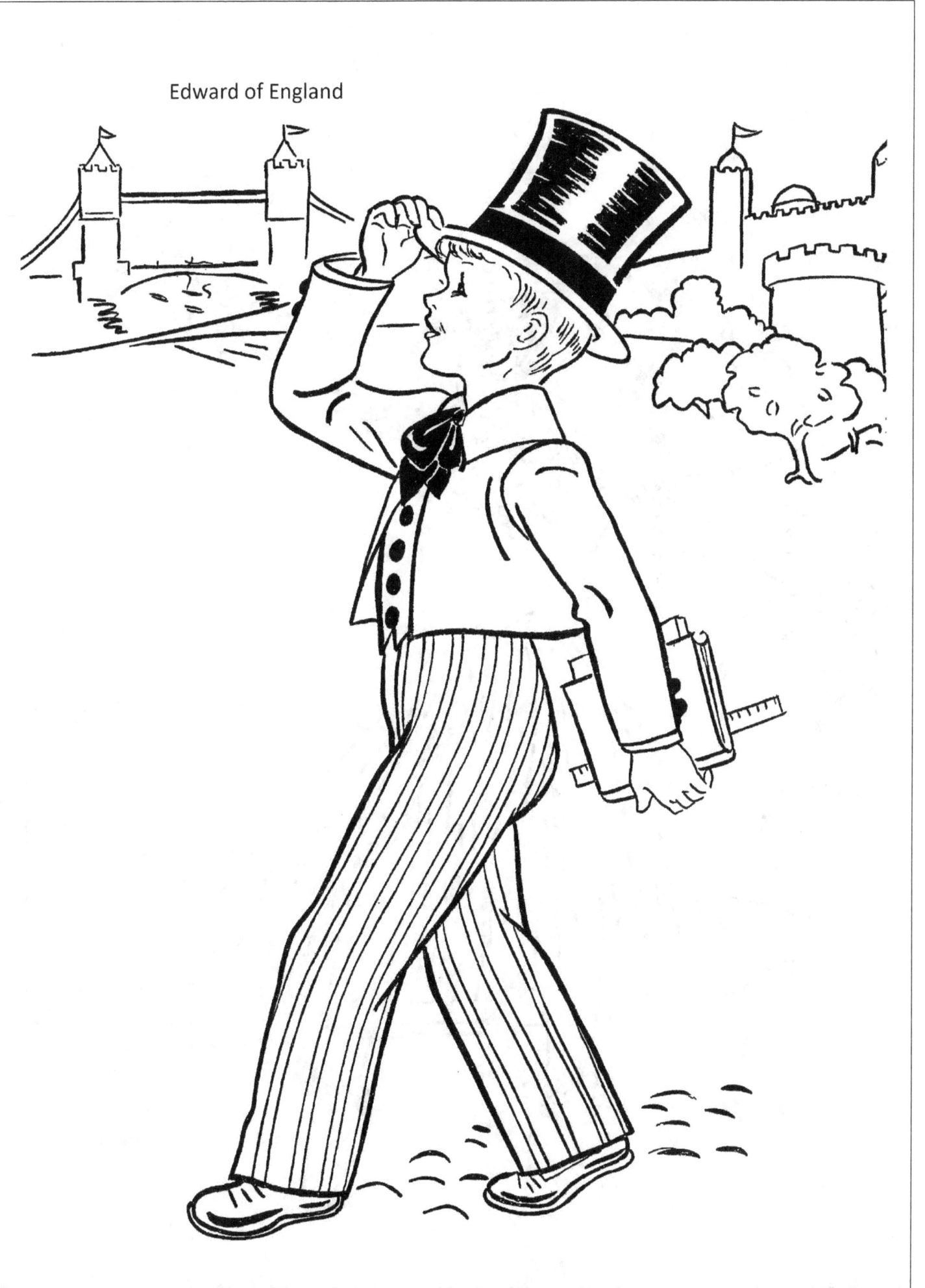

Edward of England

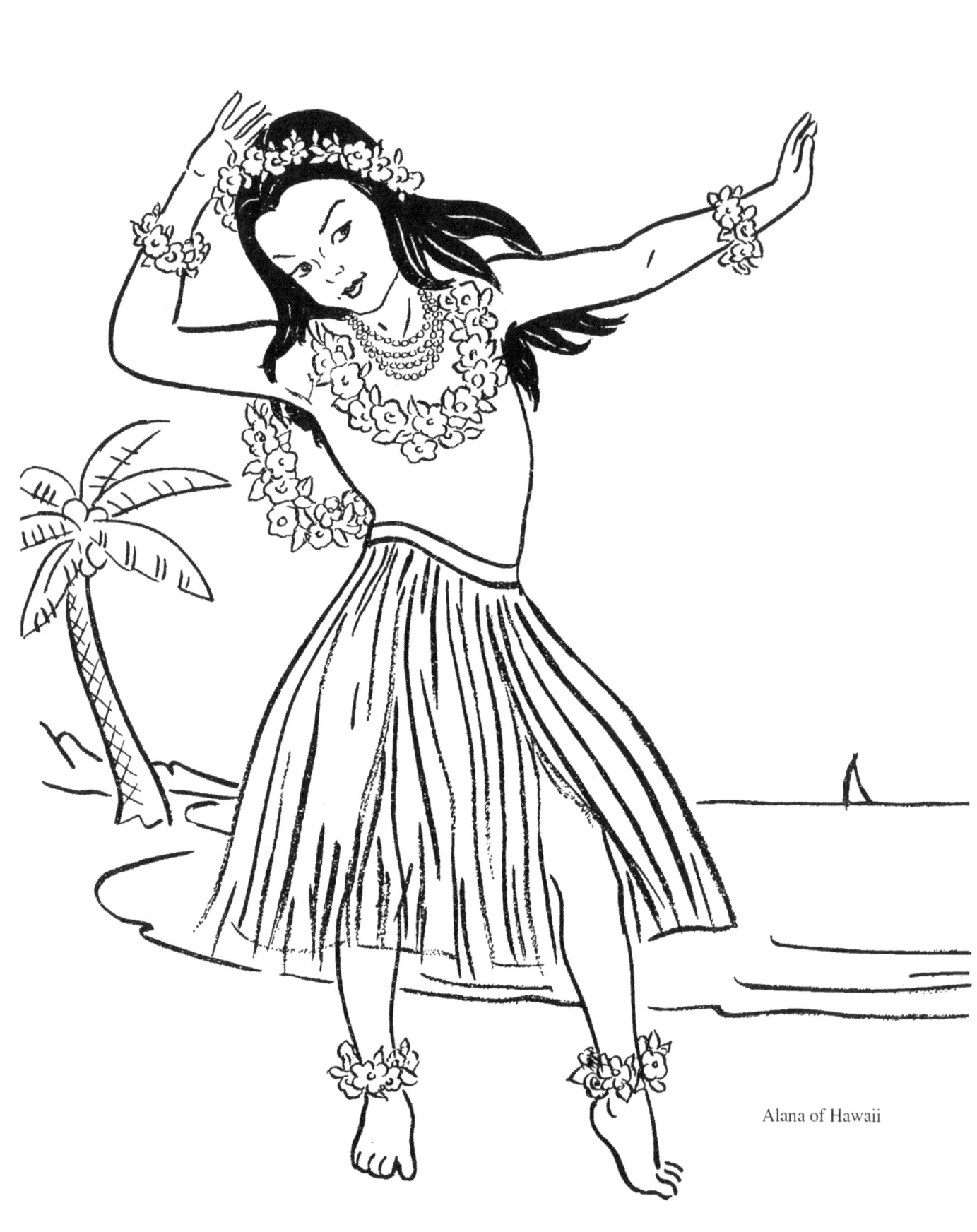

Alana of Hawaii

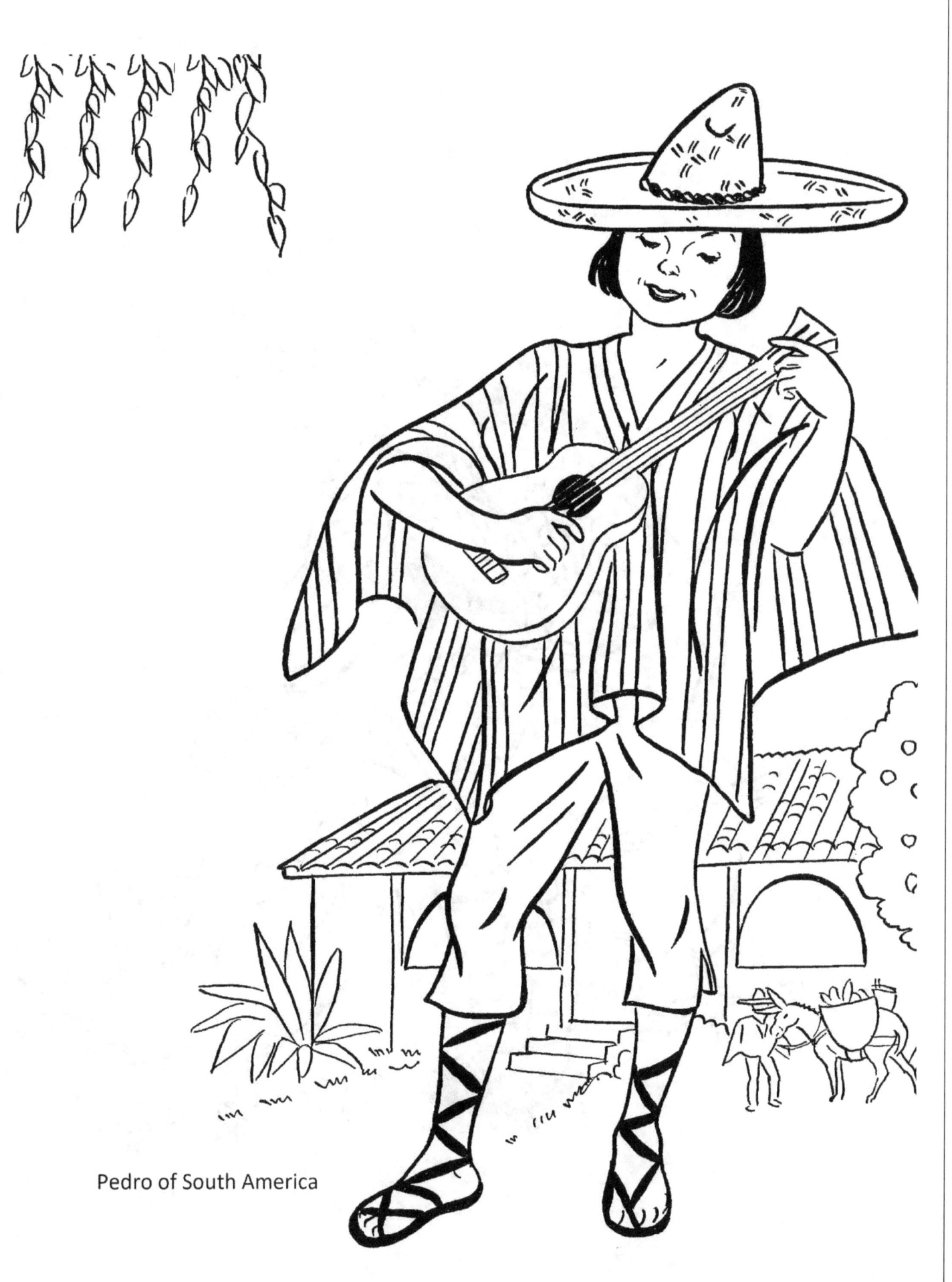

Pedro of South America

Sven of Sweden

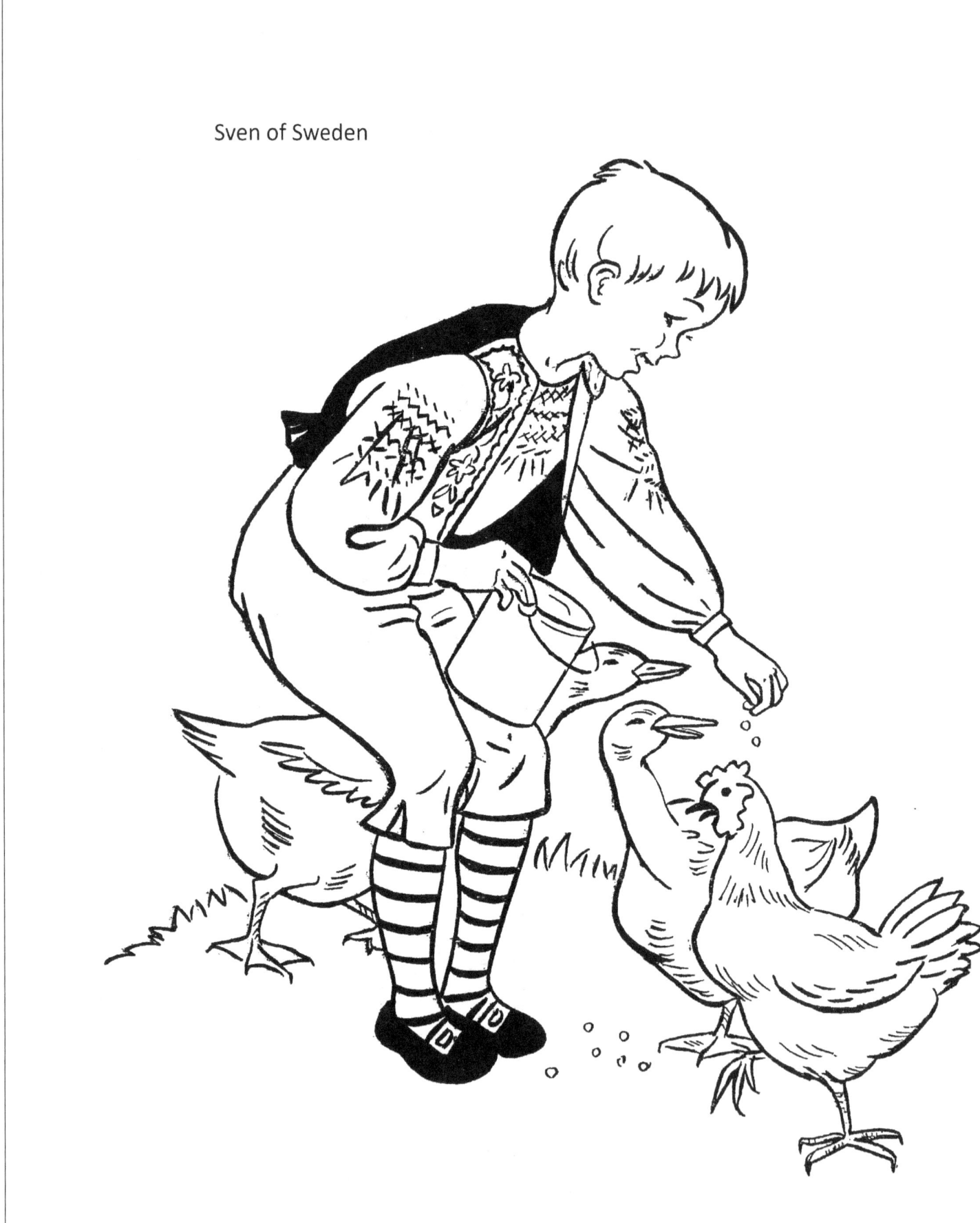

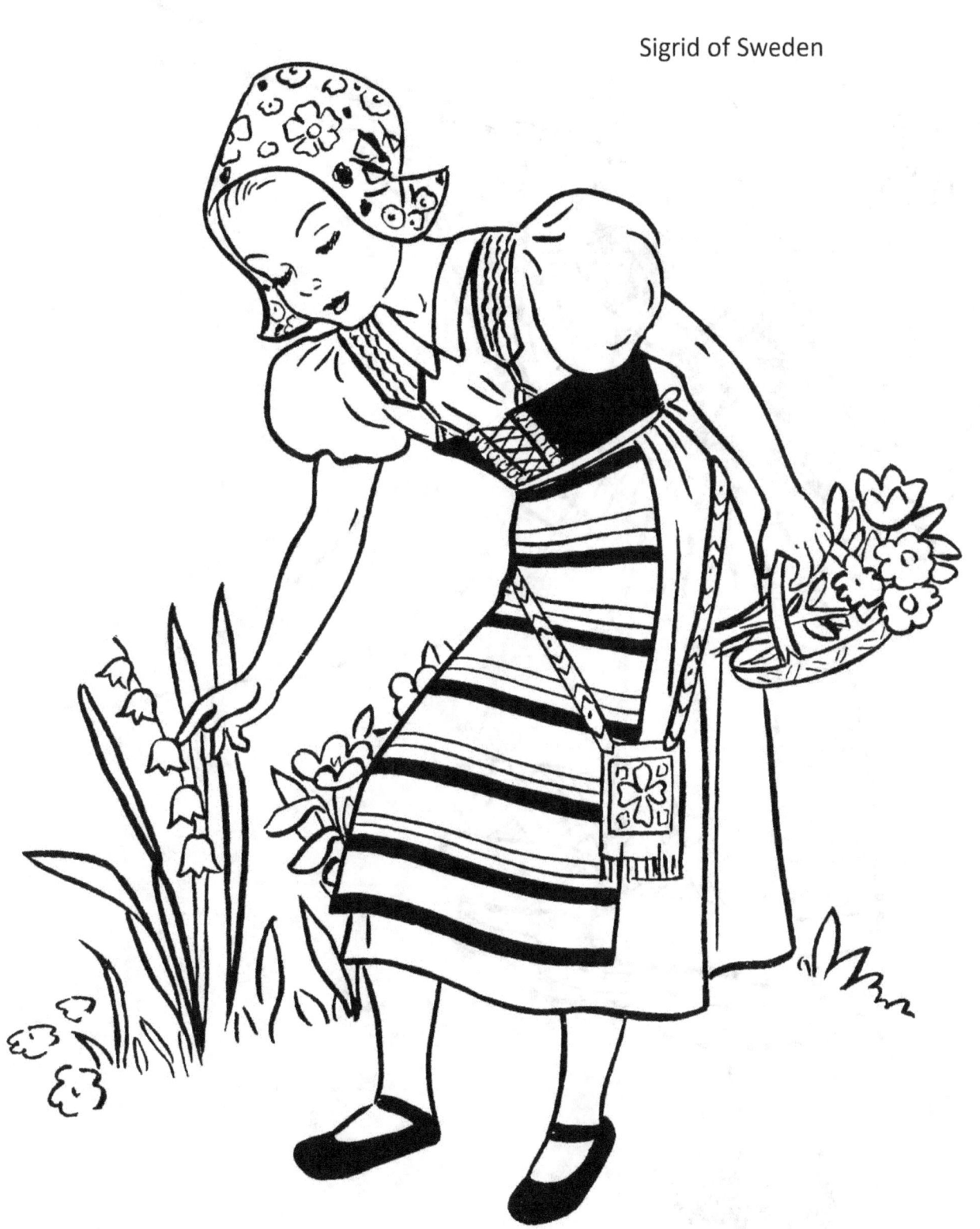

Sigrid of Sweden

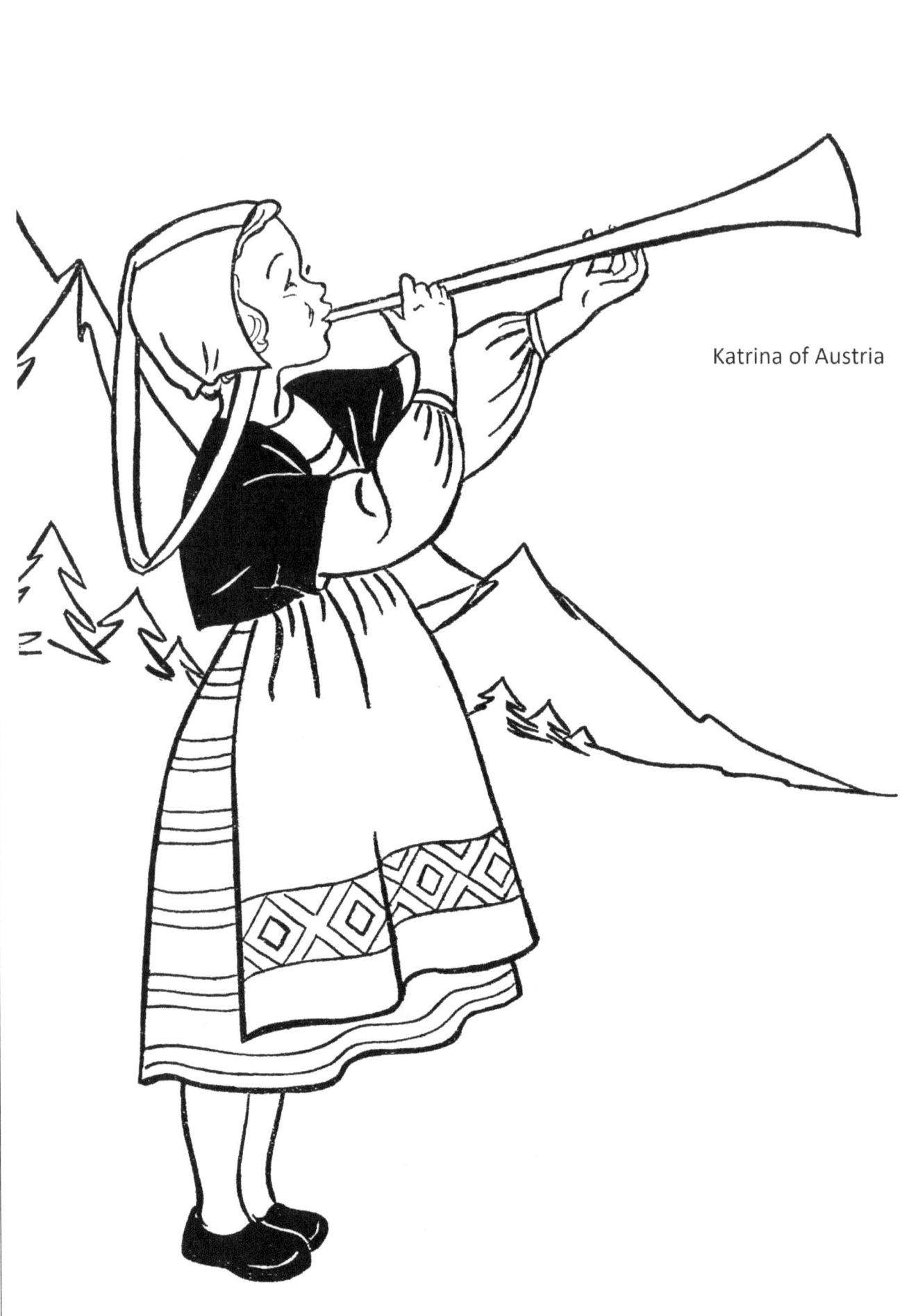

Katrina of Austria

Fritz of Austria

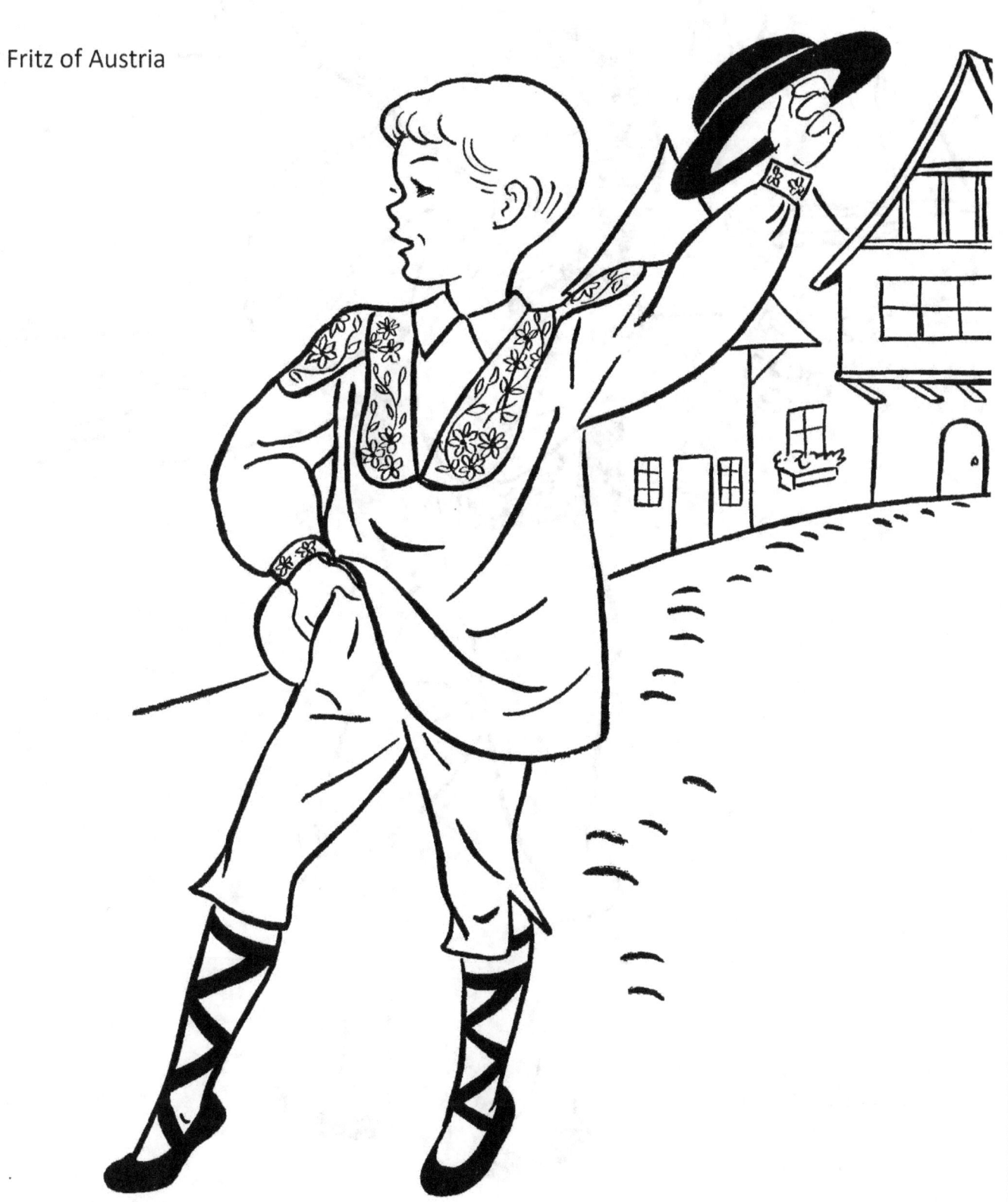

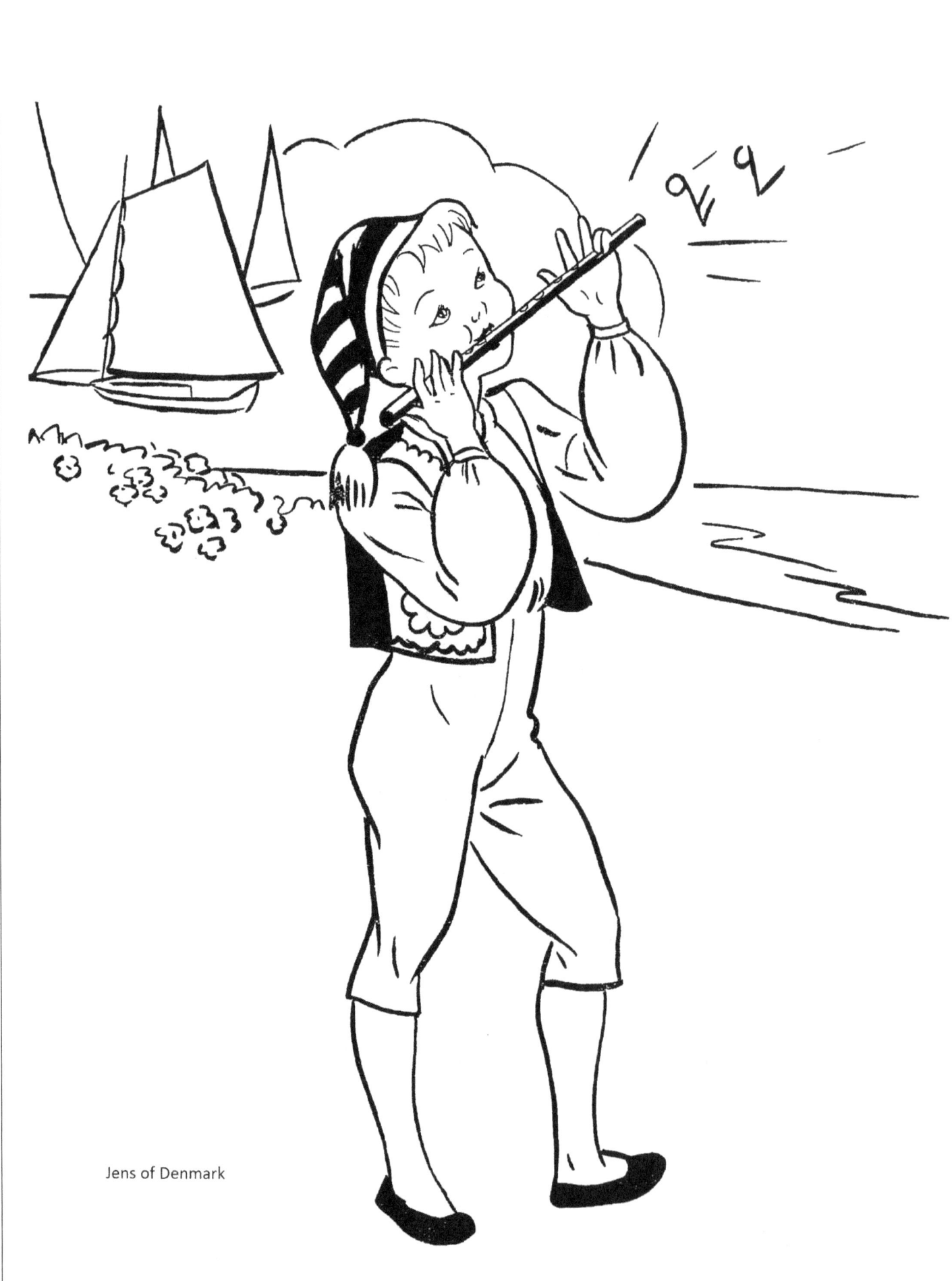

Jens of Denmark

Anna of Denmark

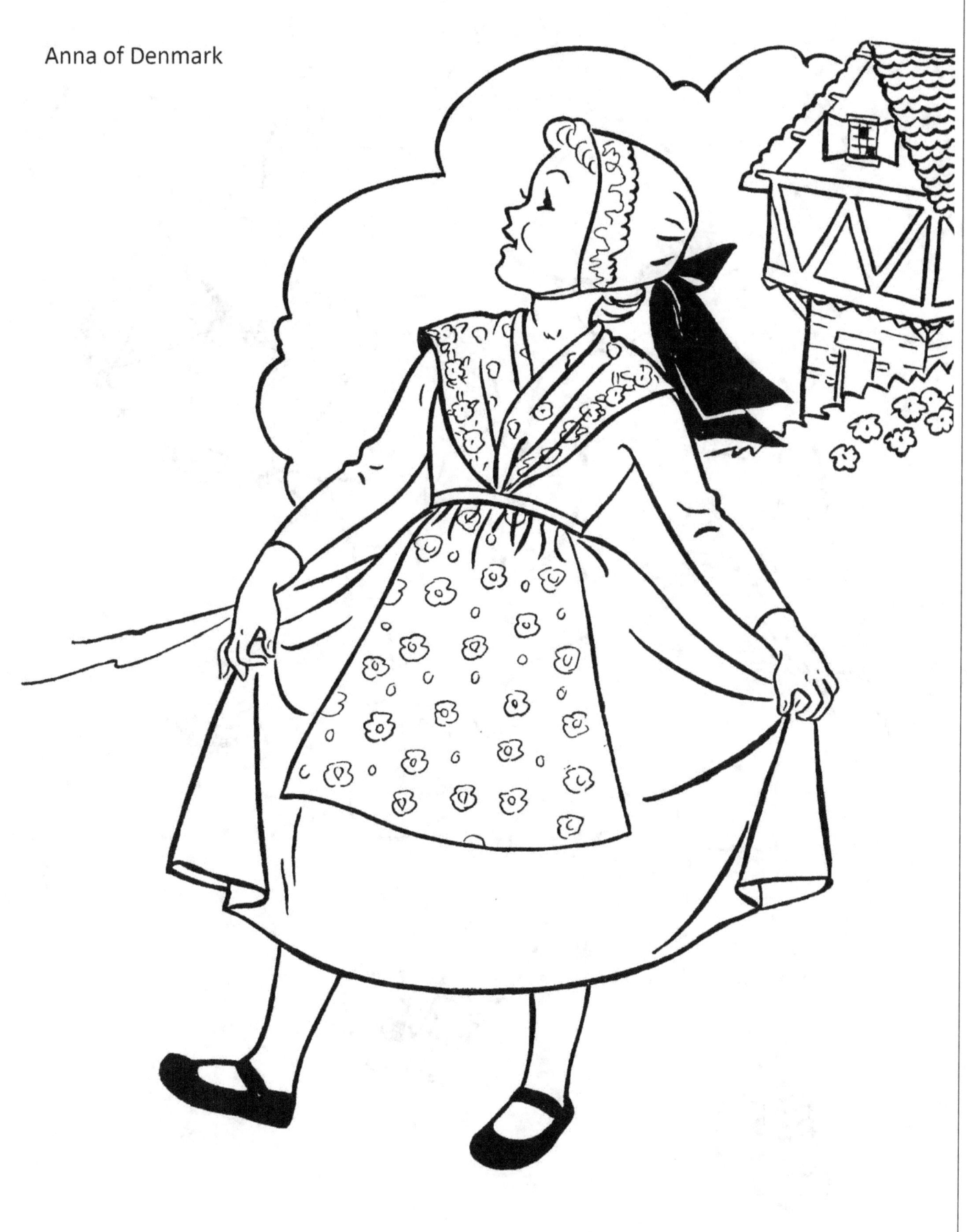

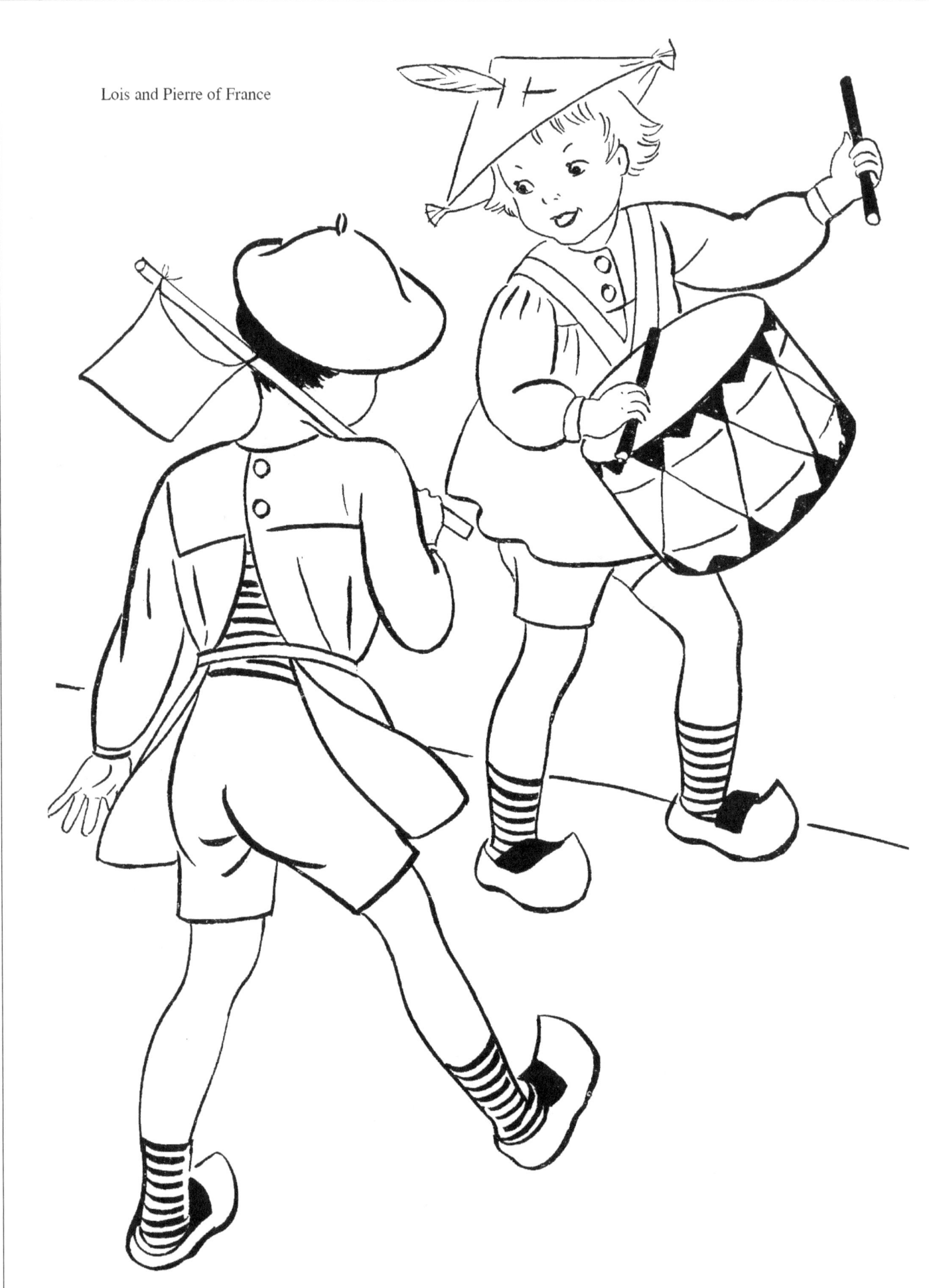

Lois and Pierre of France

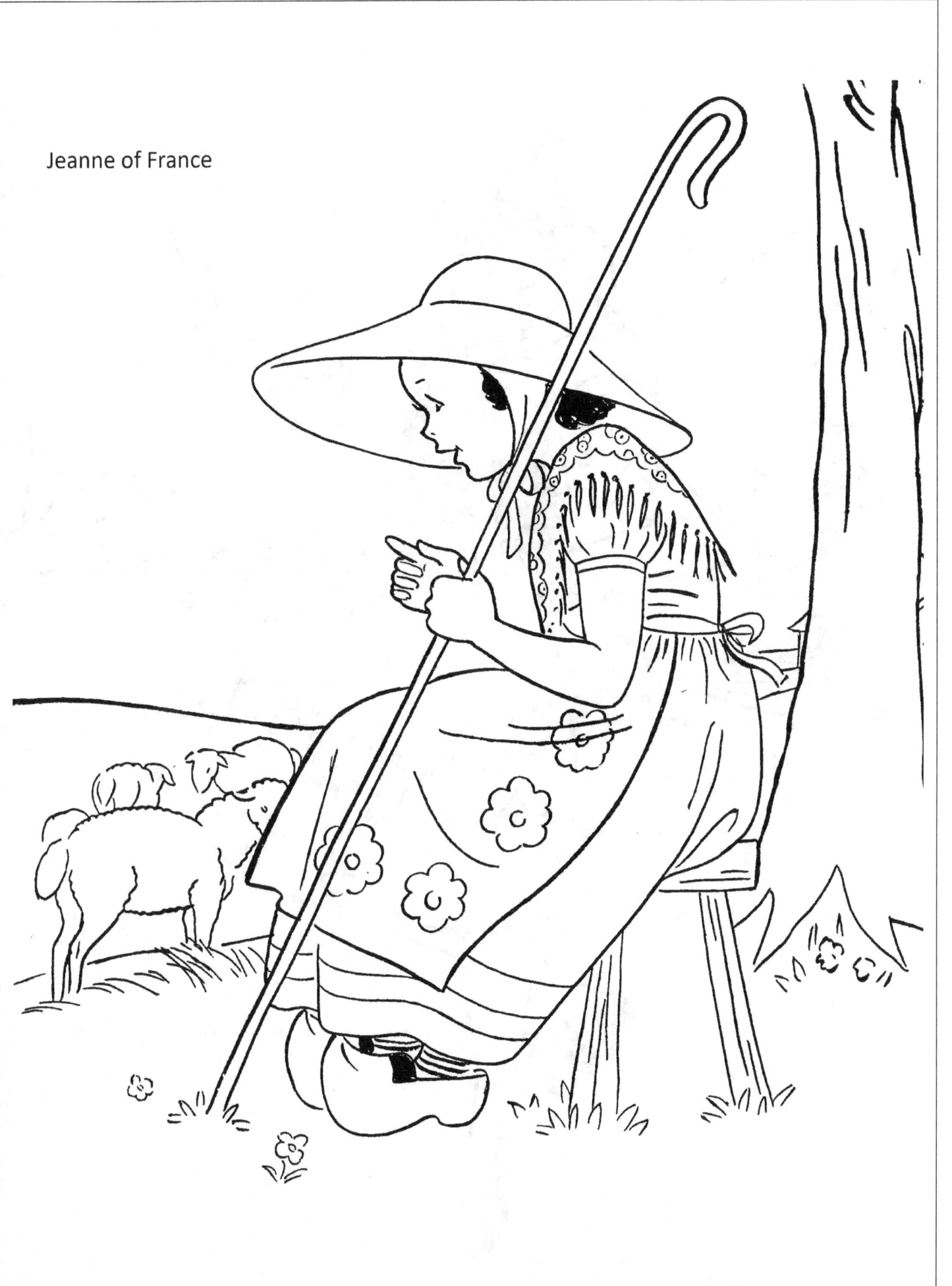

Jeanne of France

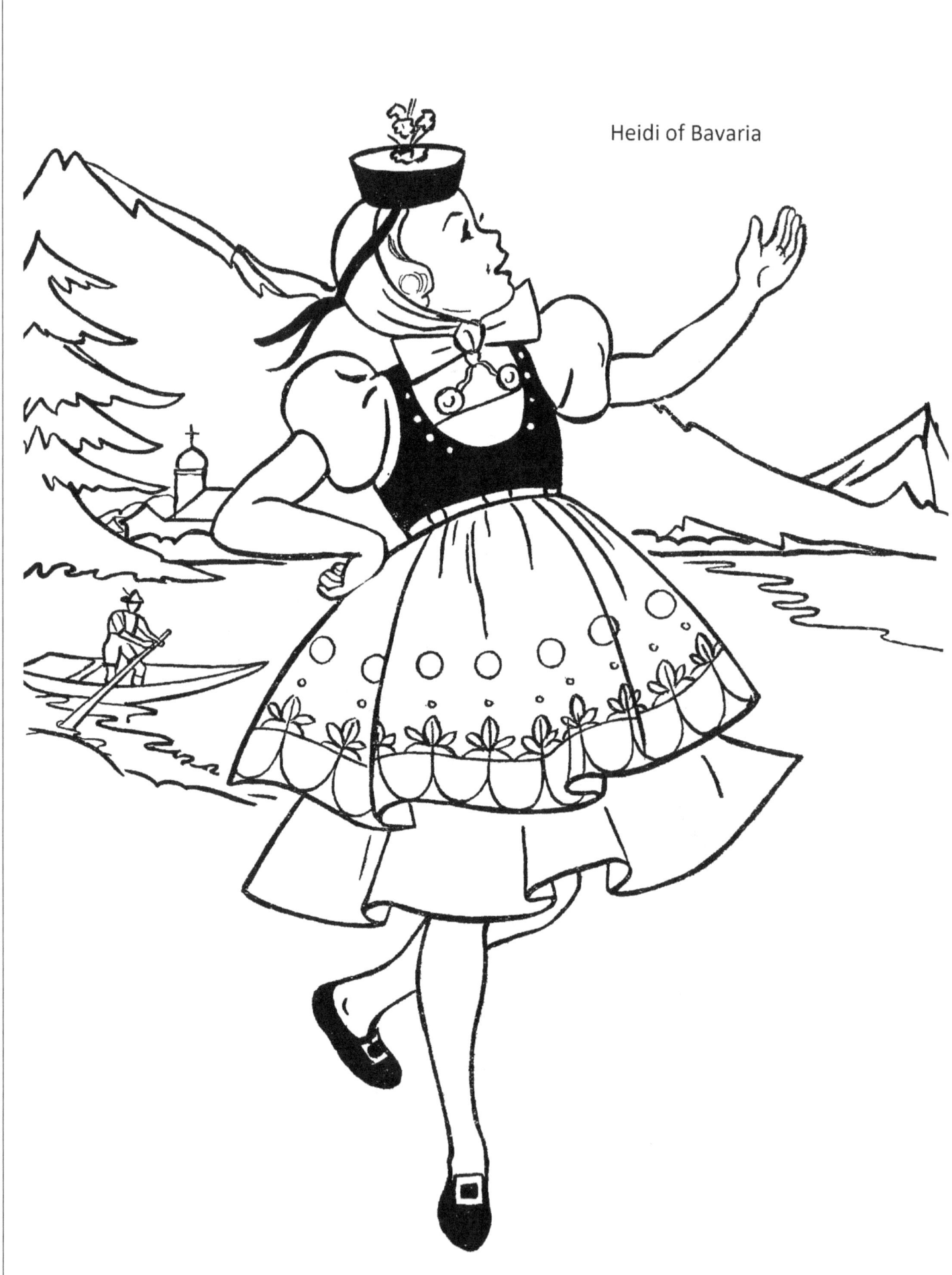

Heidi of Bavaria

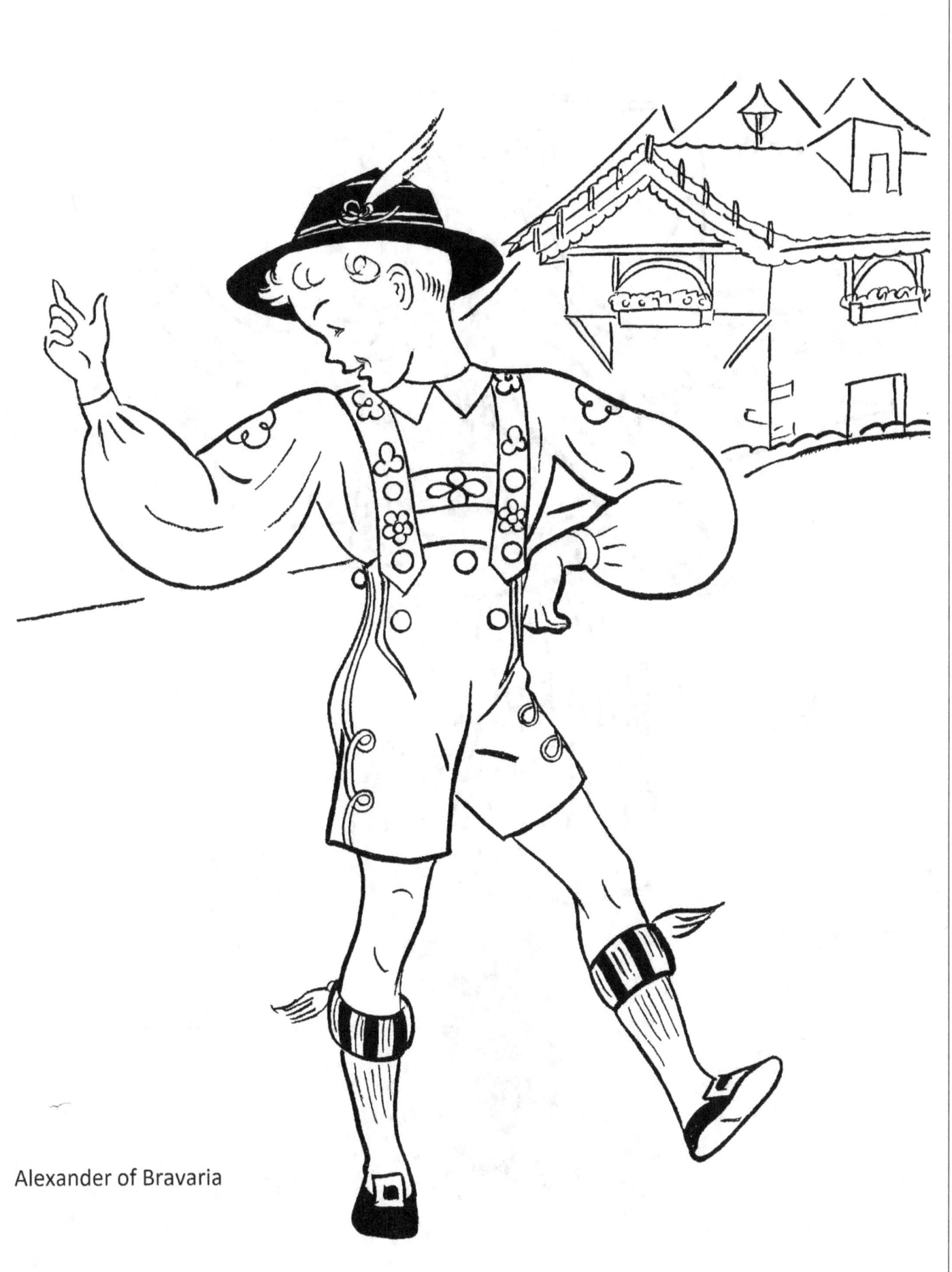

Alexander of Bravaria

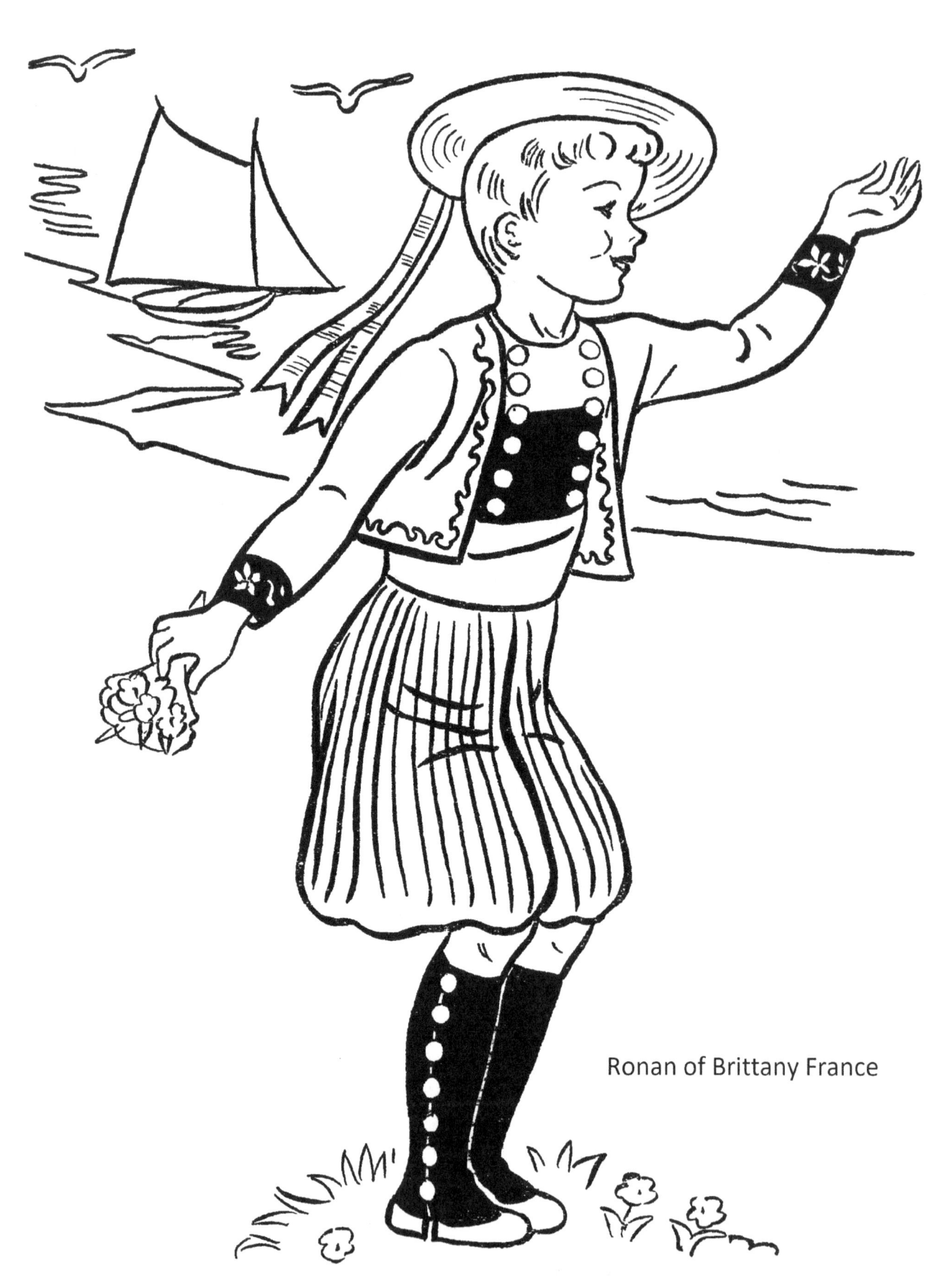

Ronan of Brittany France

Marie of Brittany France

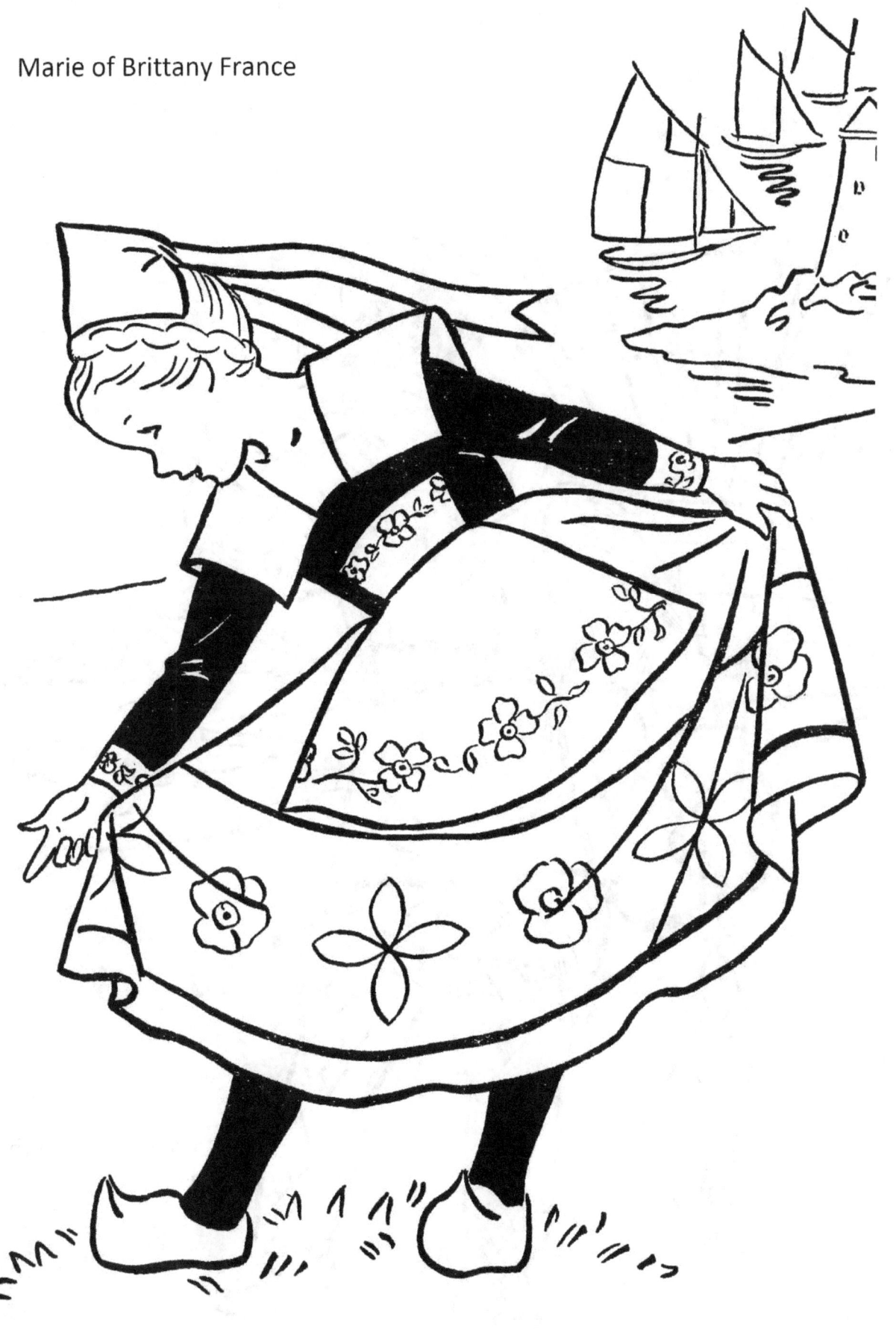

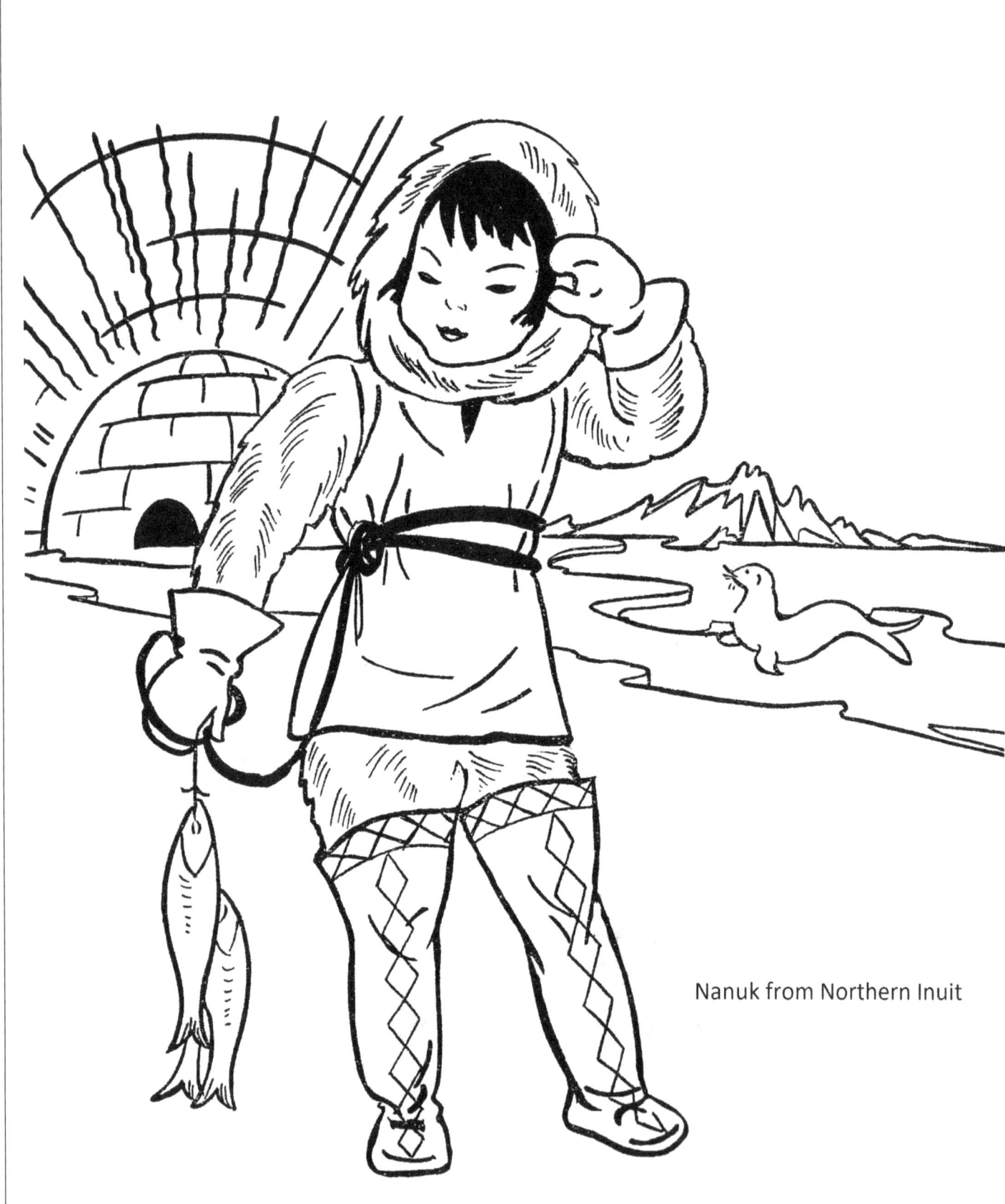

Nanuk from Northern Inuit

Erik of Greenland

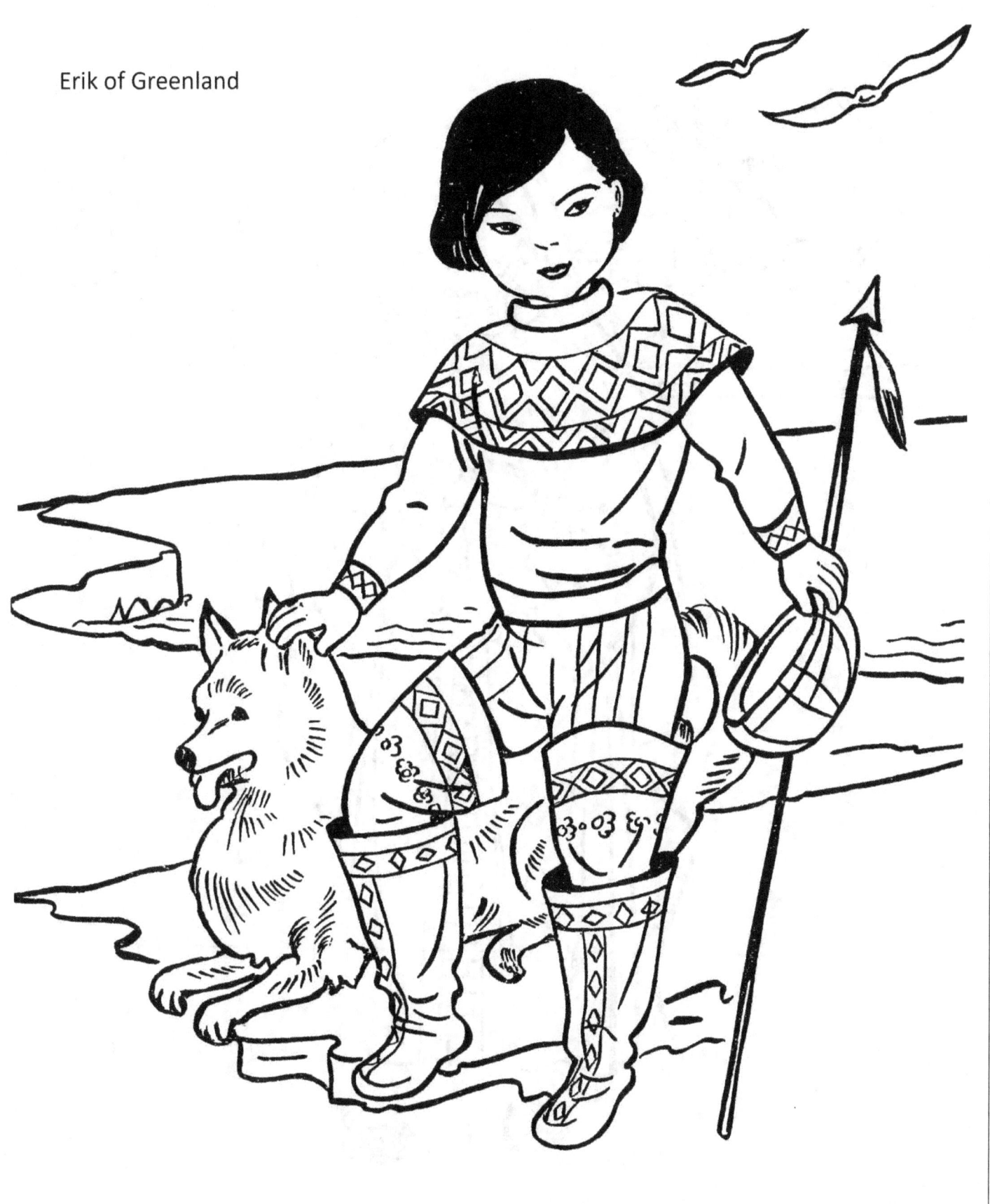

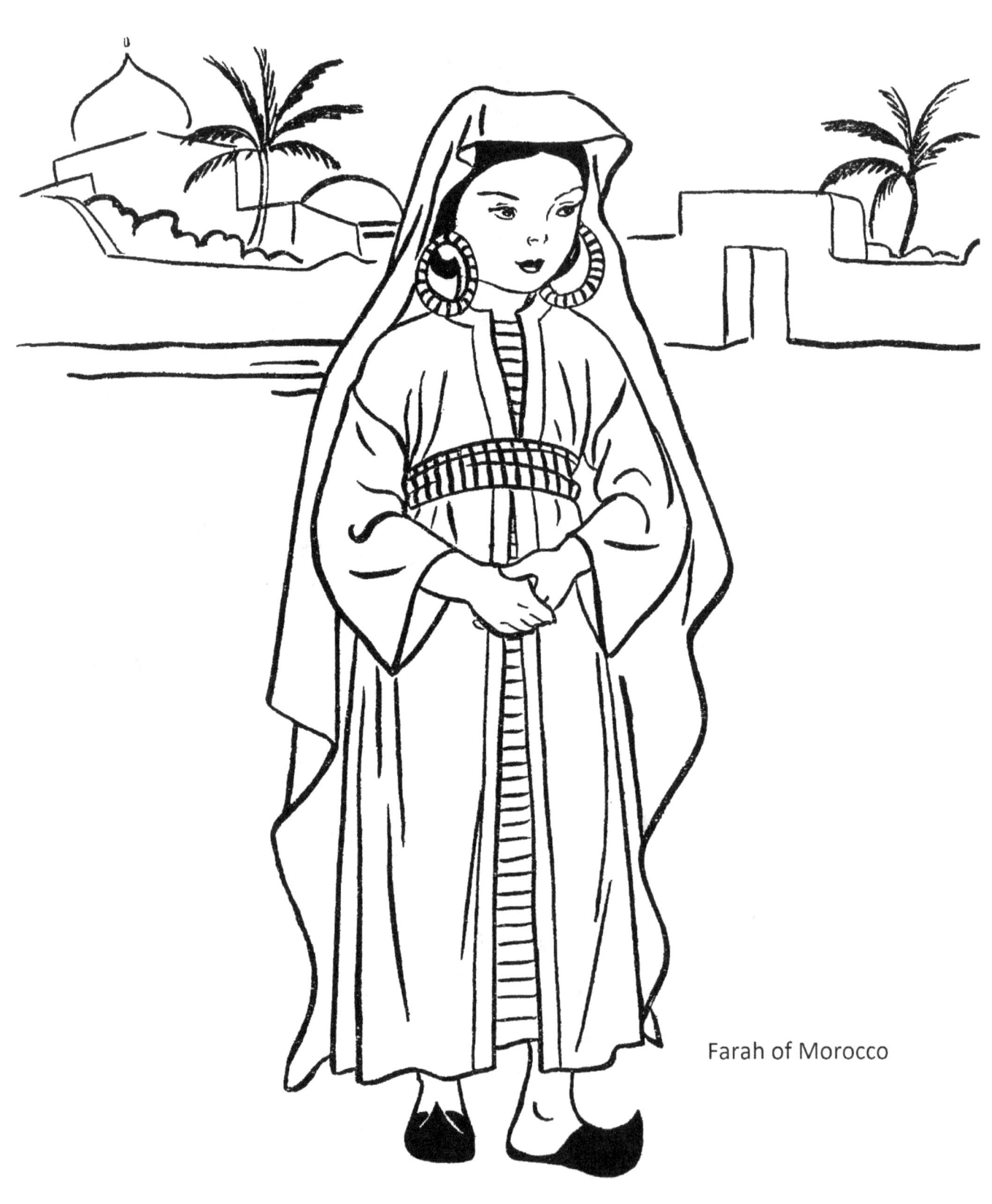

Farah of Morocco

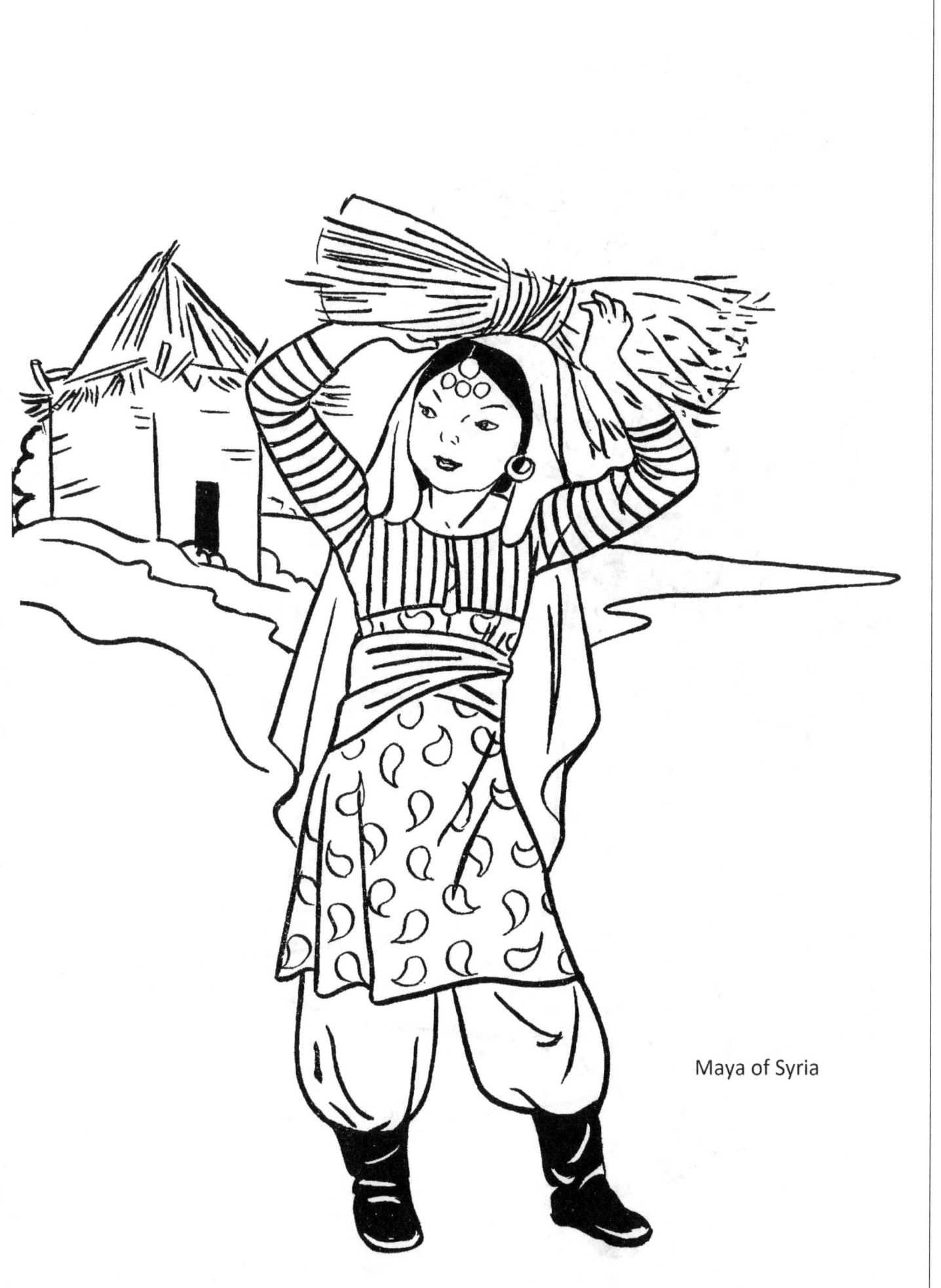

Maya of Syria

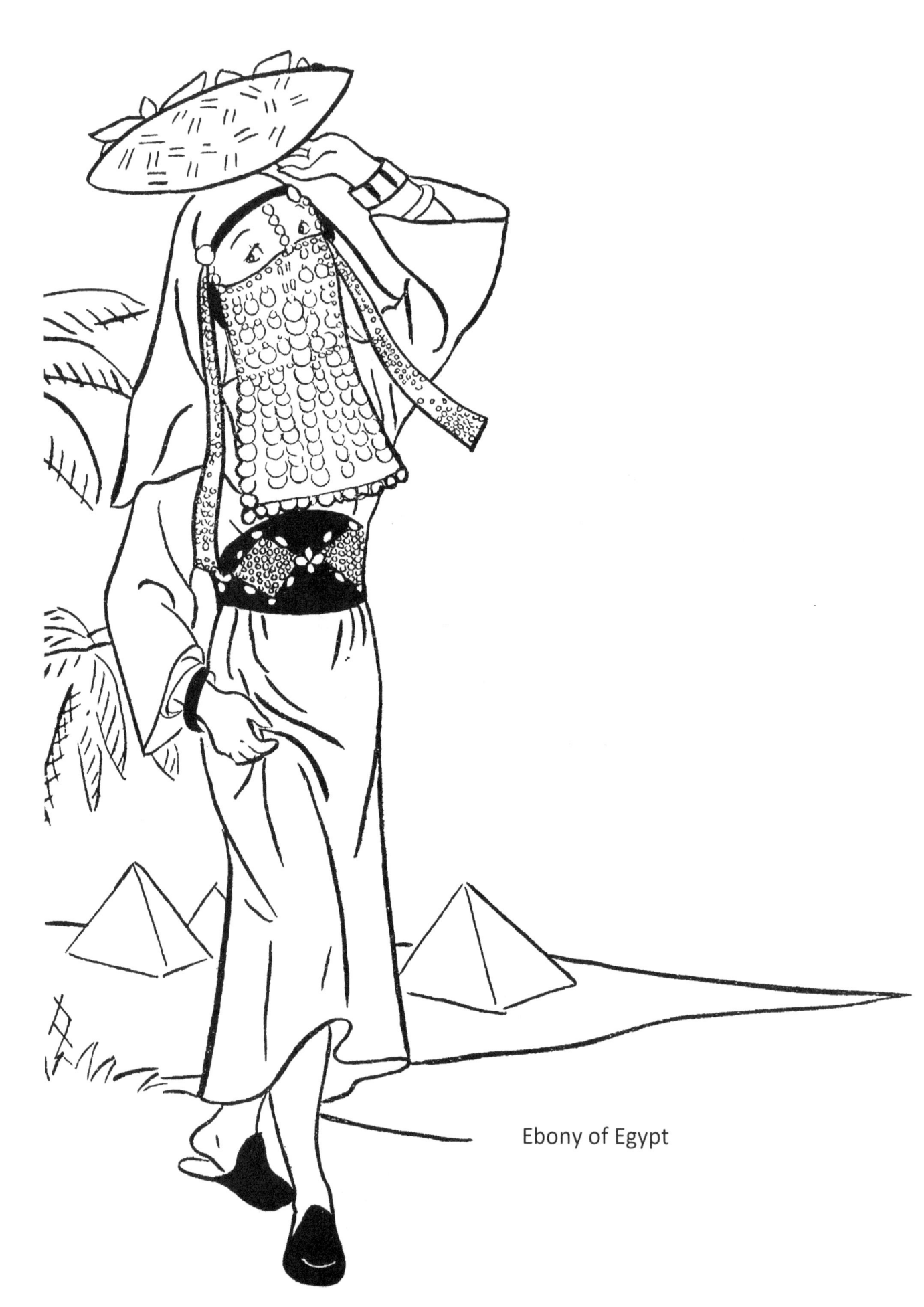

Ebony of Egypt

Jasper of Persia

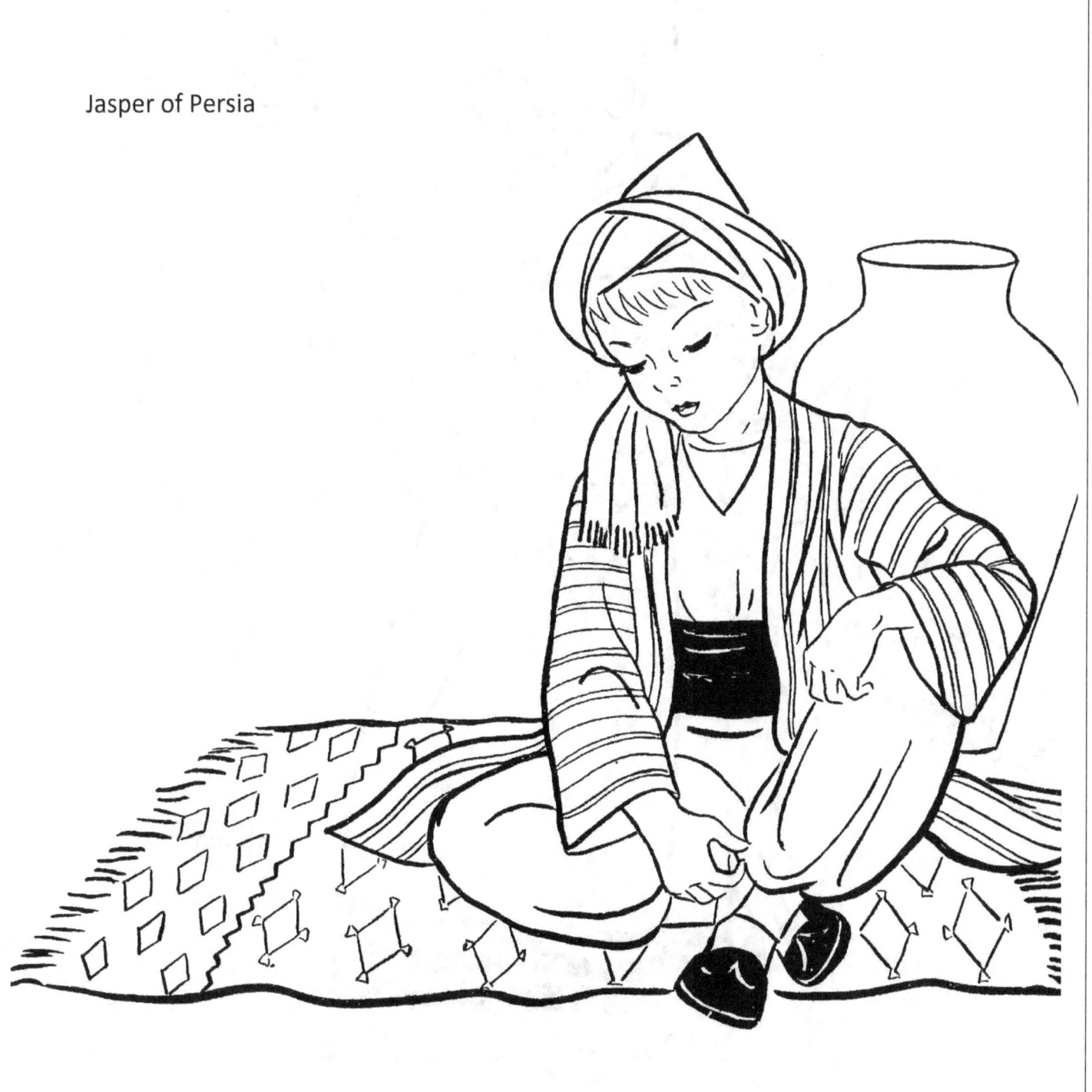

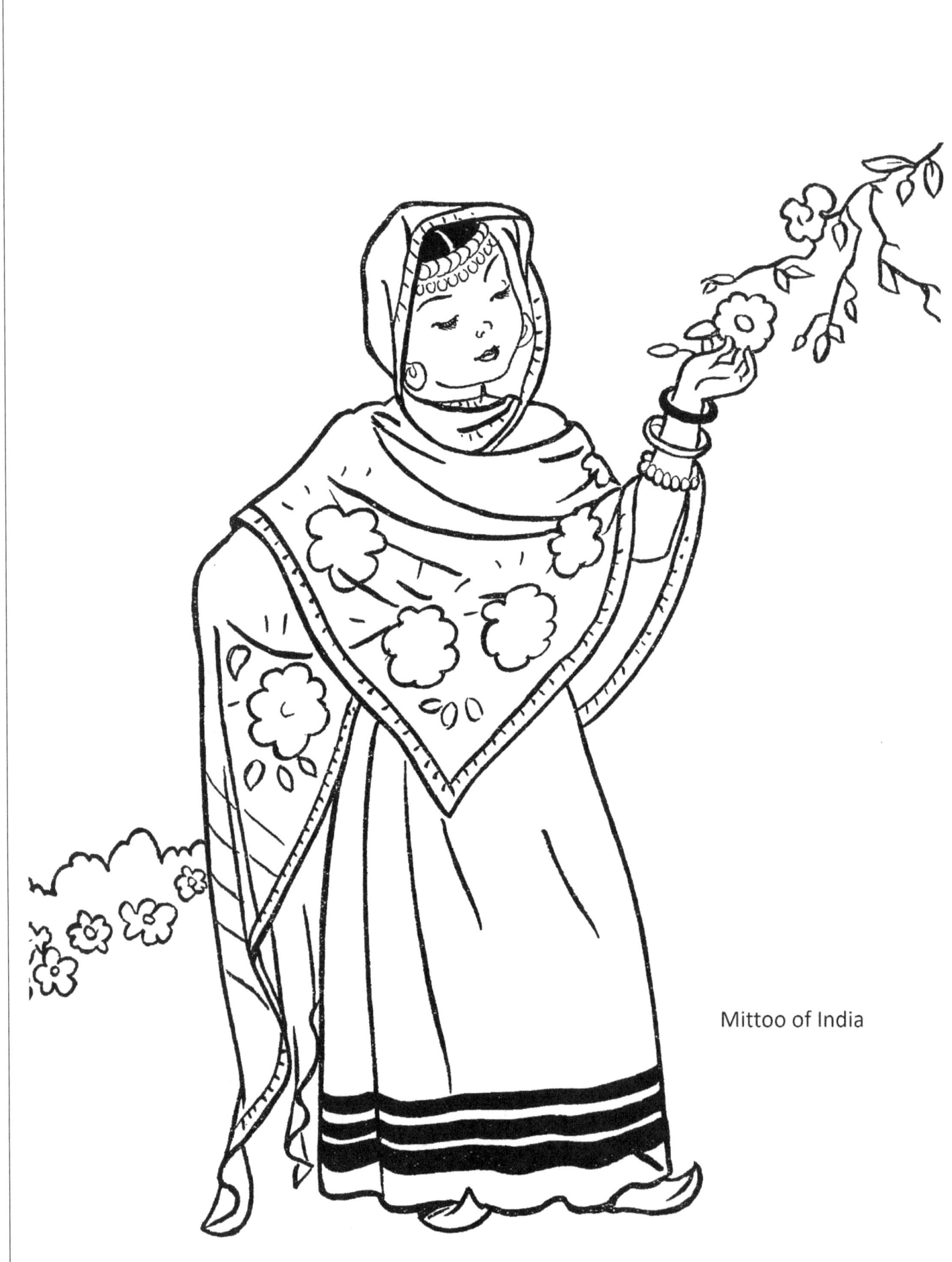

Mittoo of India

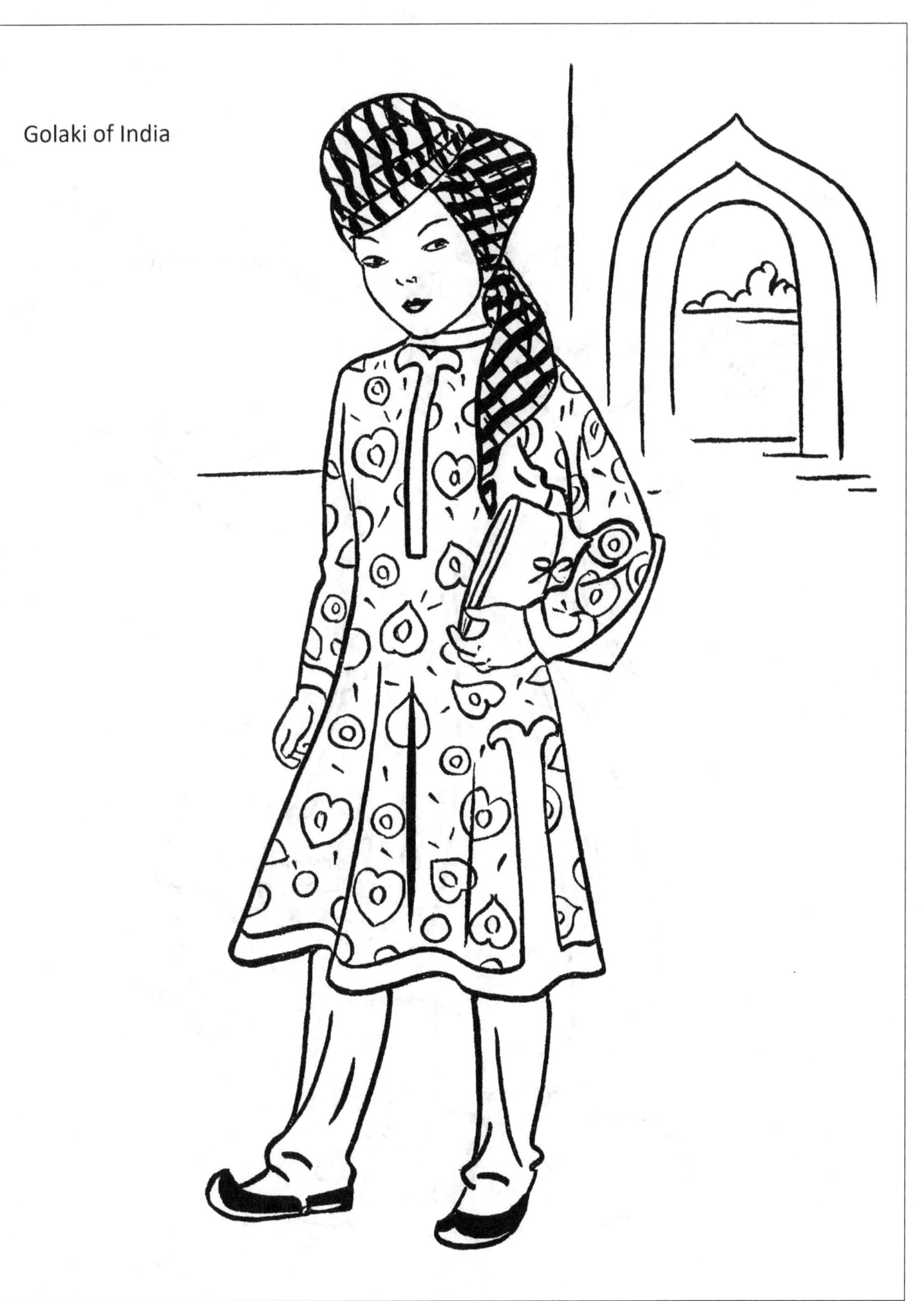

Golaki of India

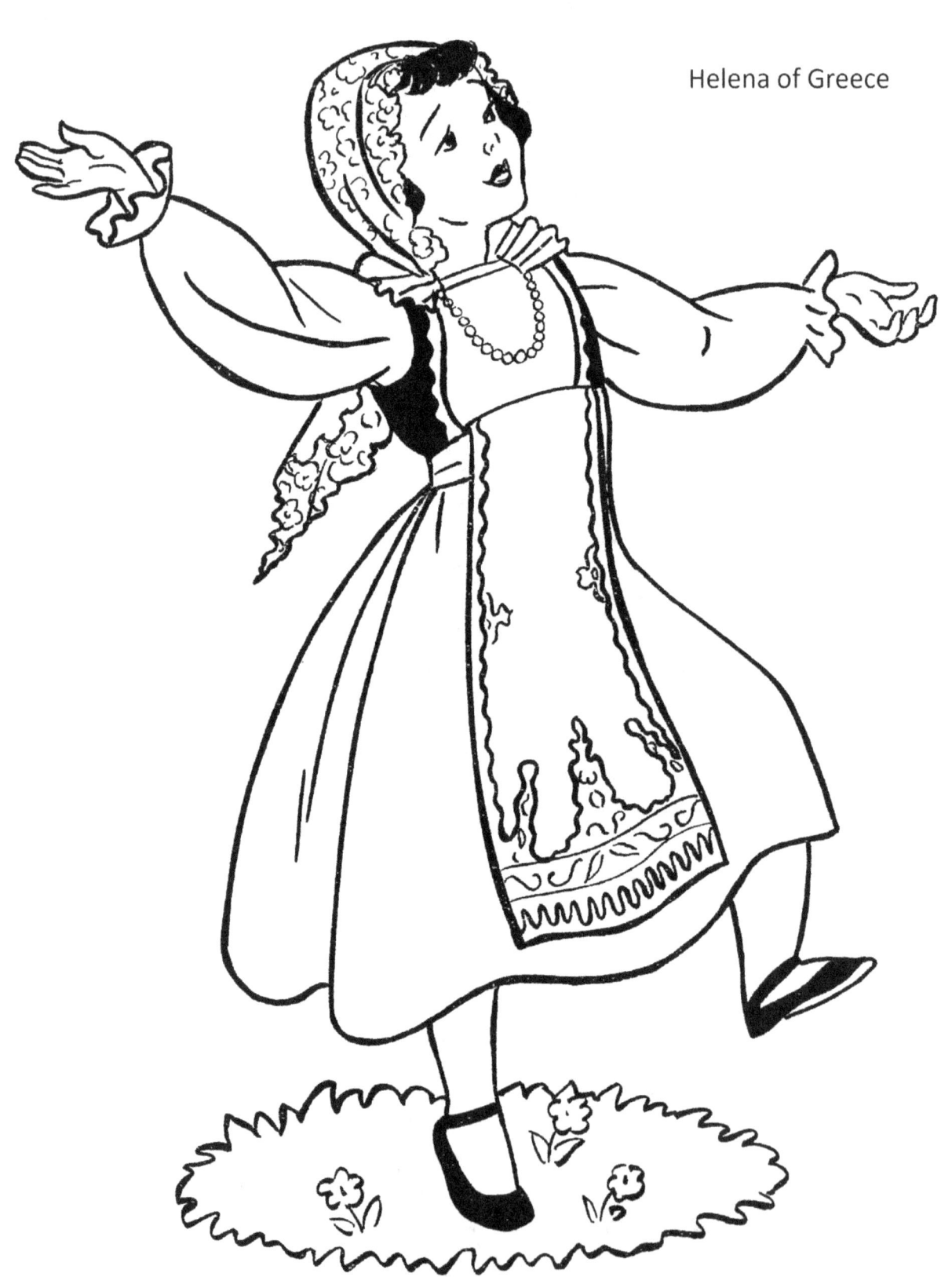

Helena of Greece

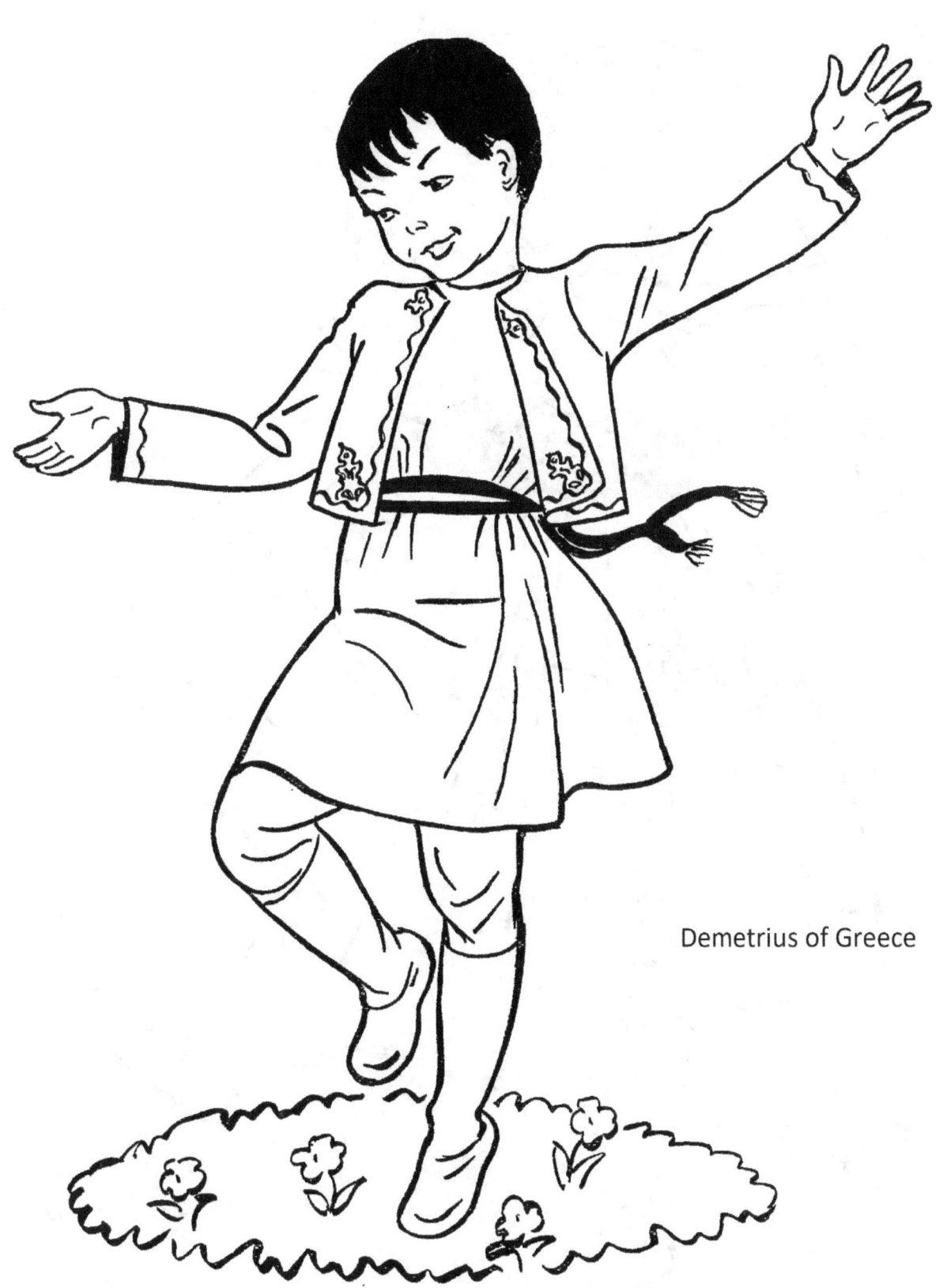

Demetrius of Greece

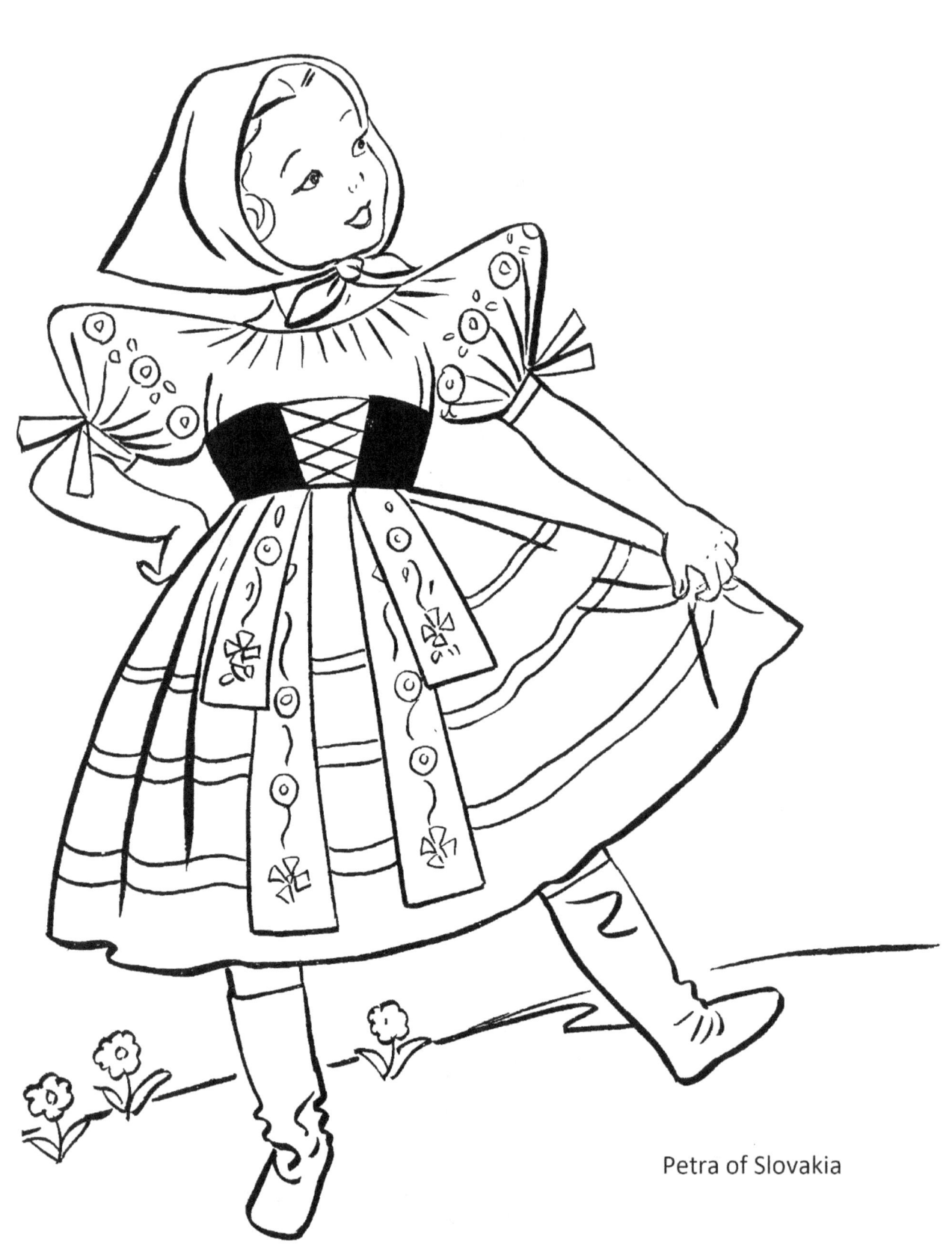

Petra of Slovakia

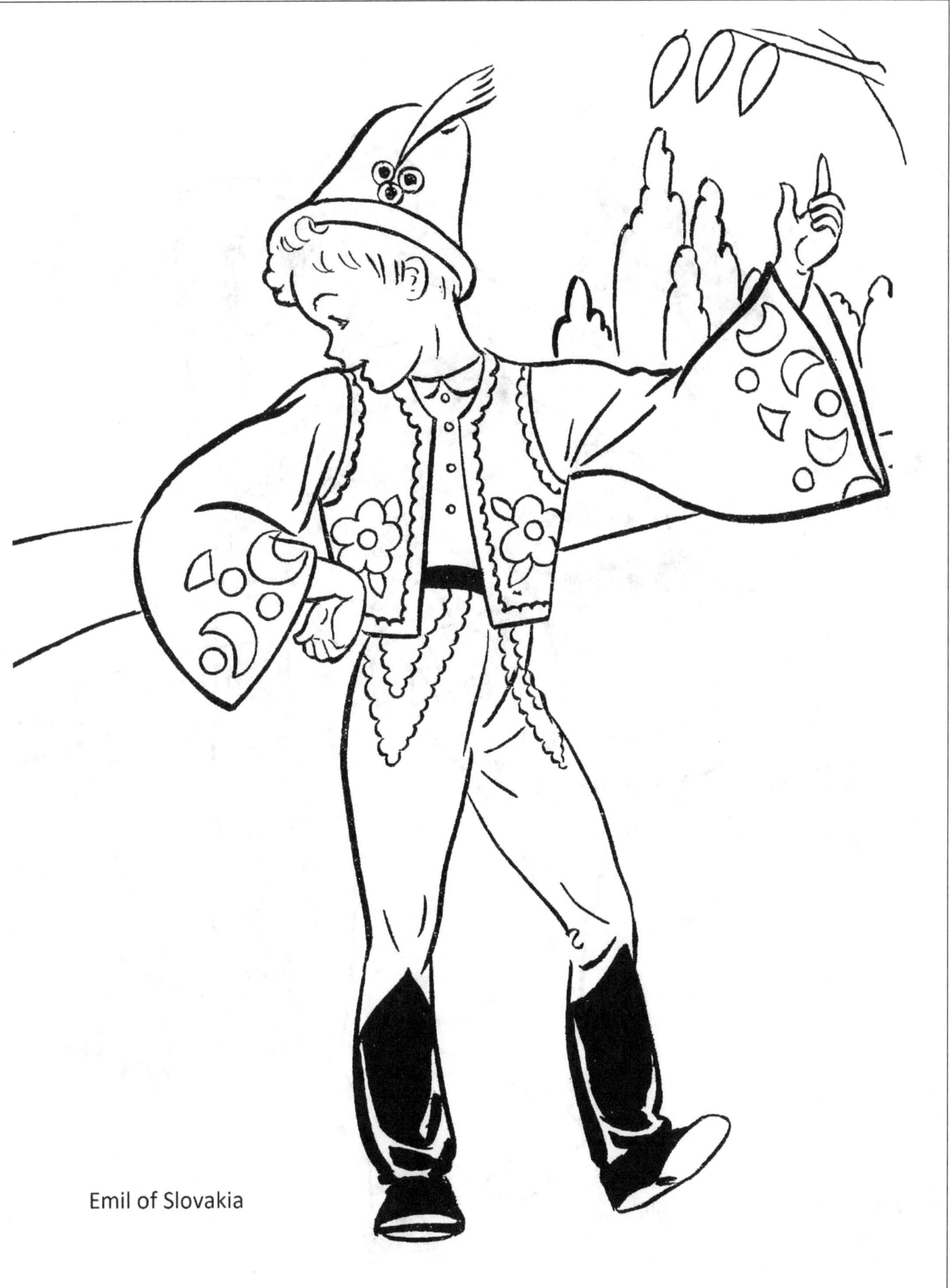

Emil of Slovakia

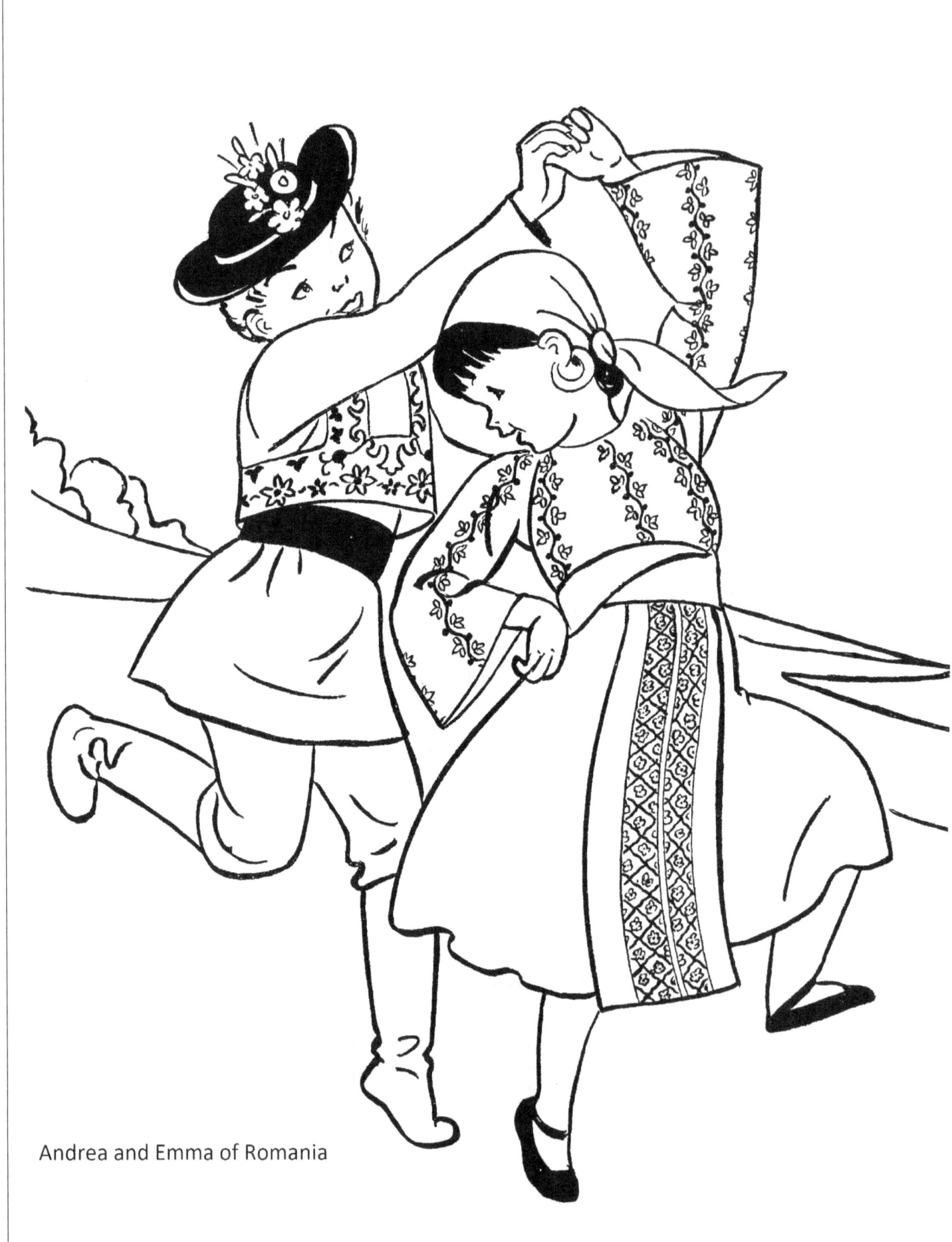

Andrea and Emma of Romania

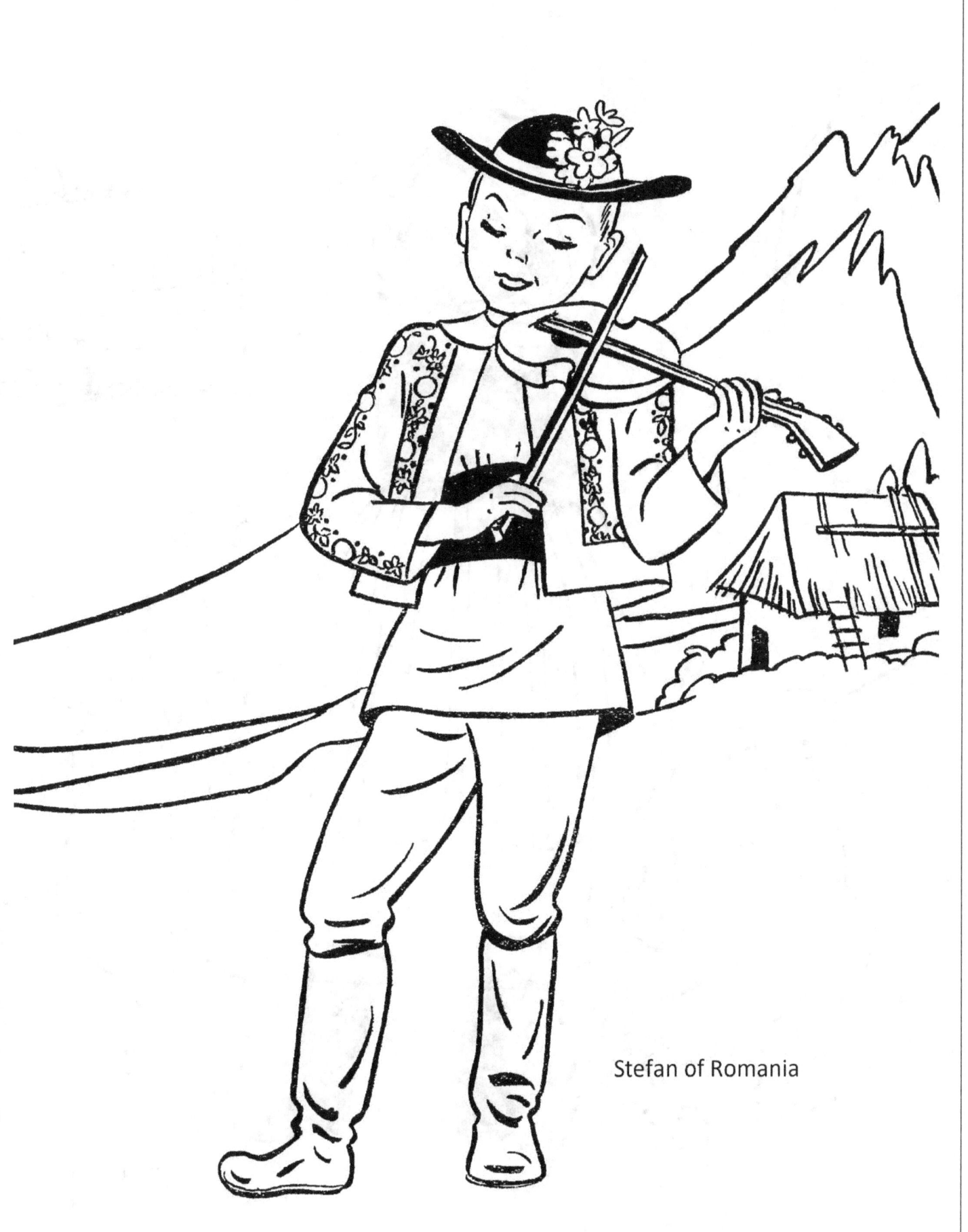

Stefan of Romania

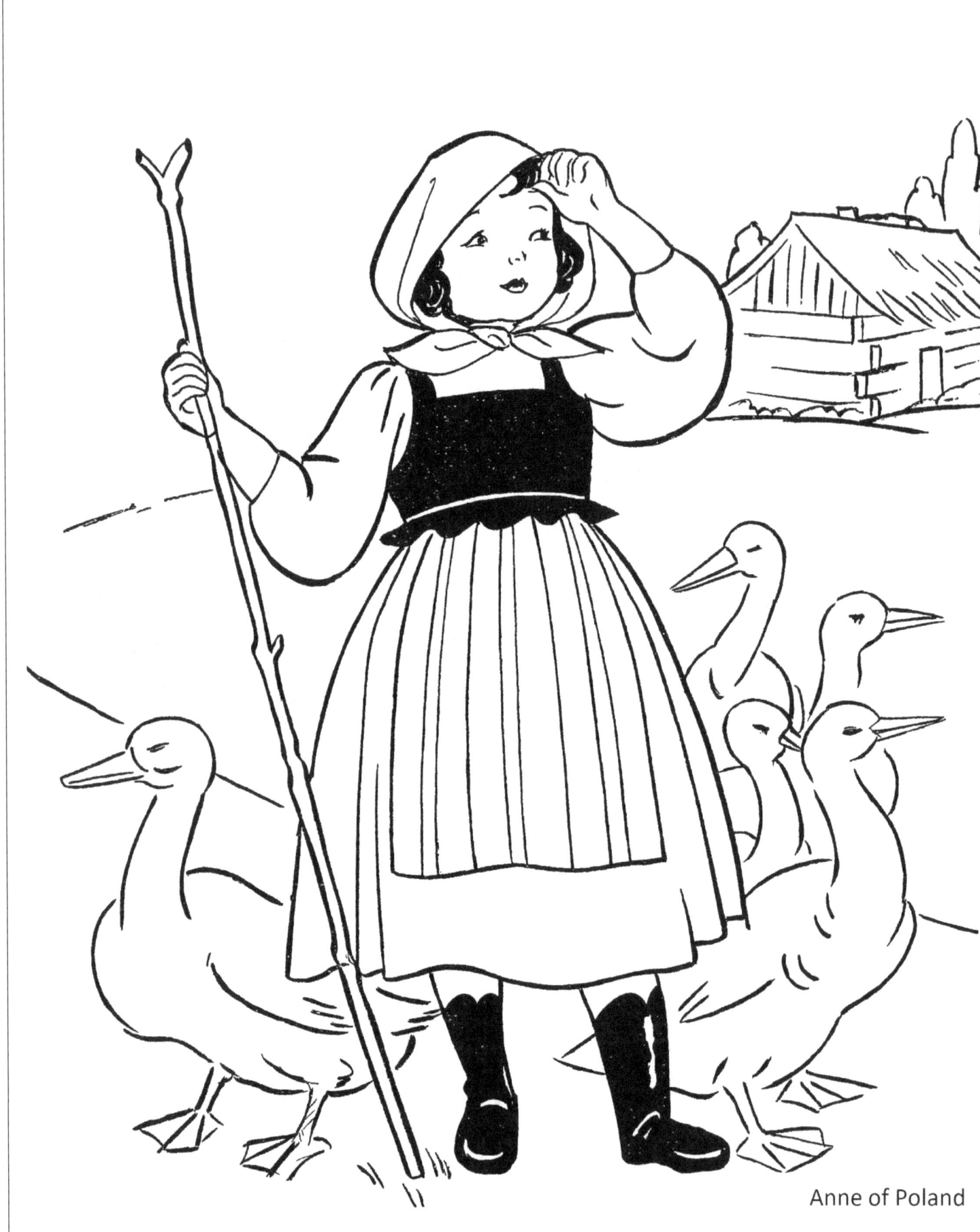

Anne of Poland

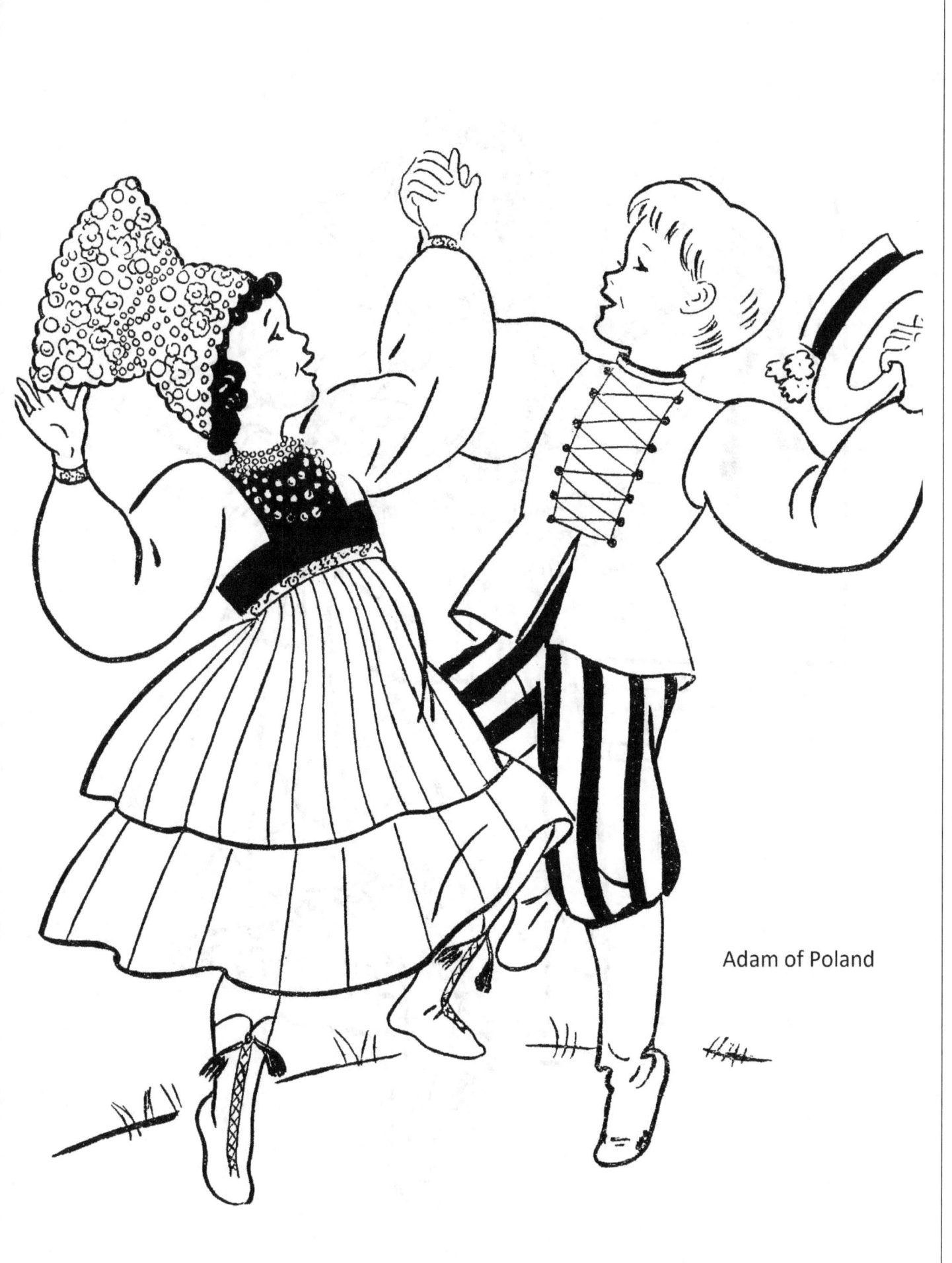

Adam of Poland

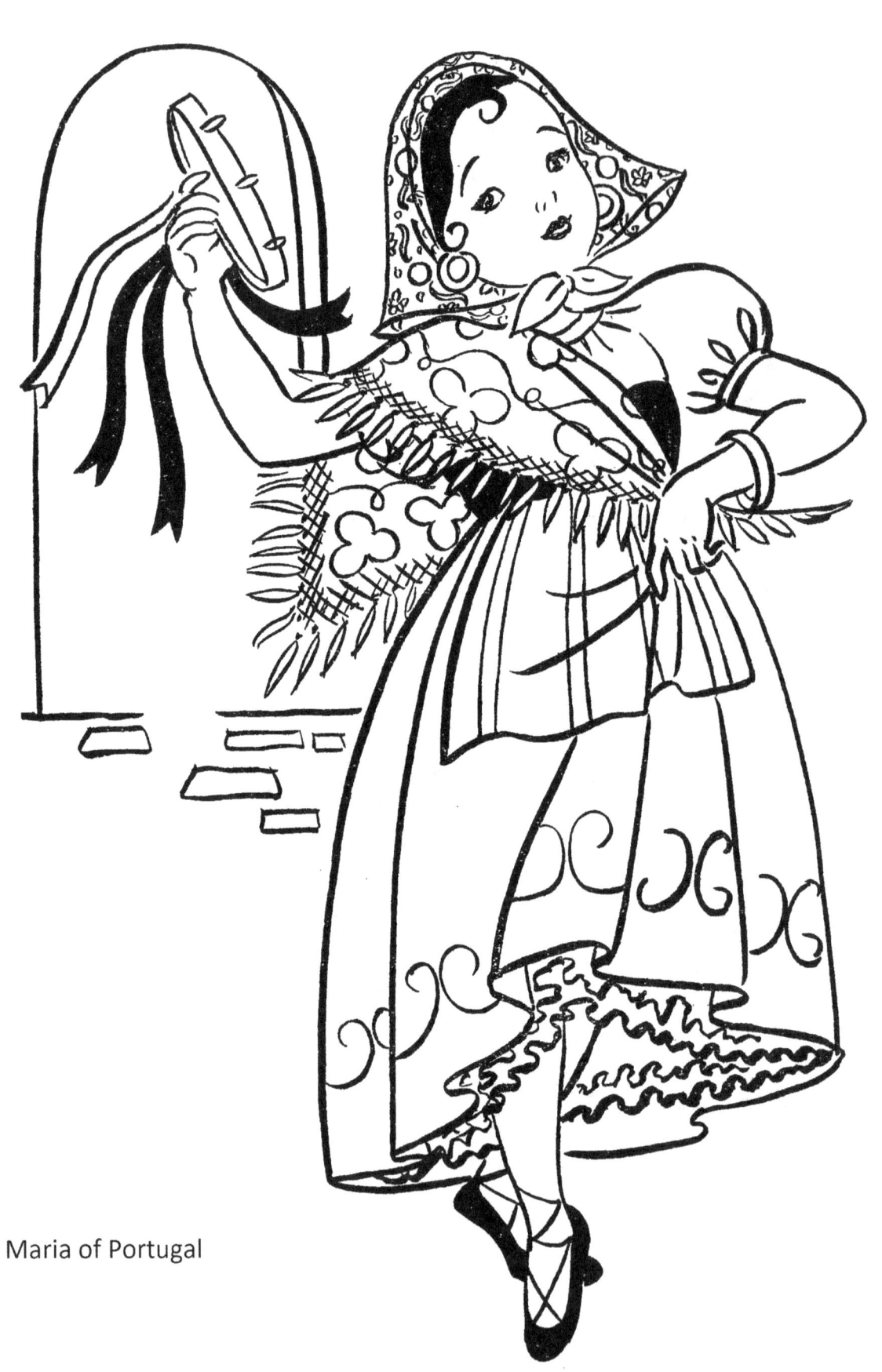

Maria of Portugal

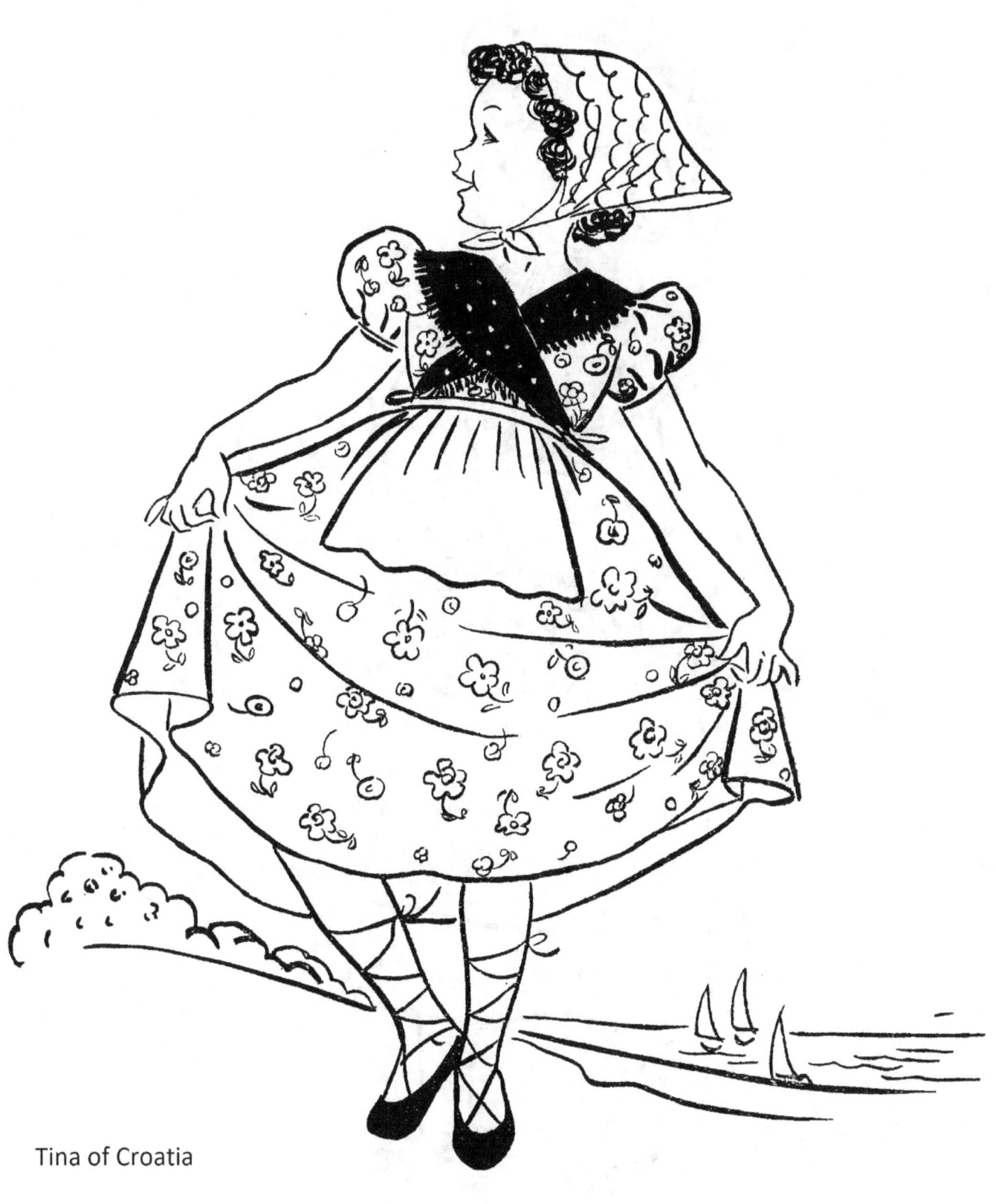

Tina of Croatia

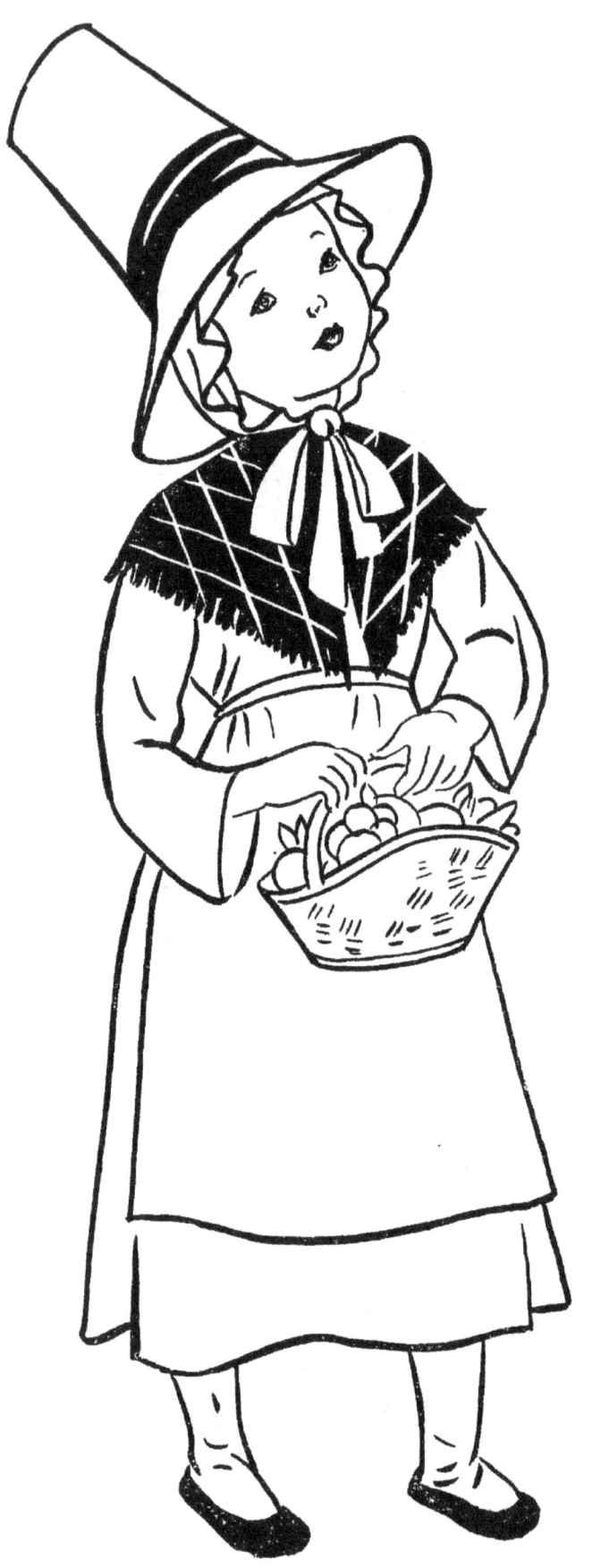

Glennis of Wales

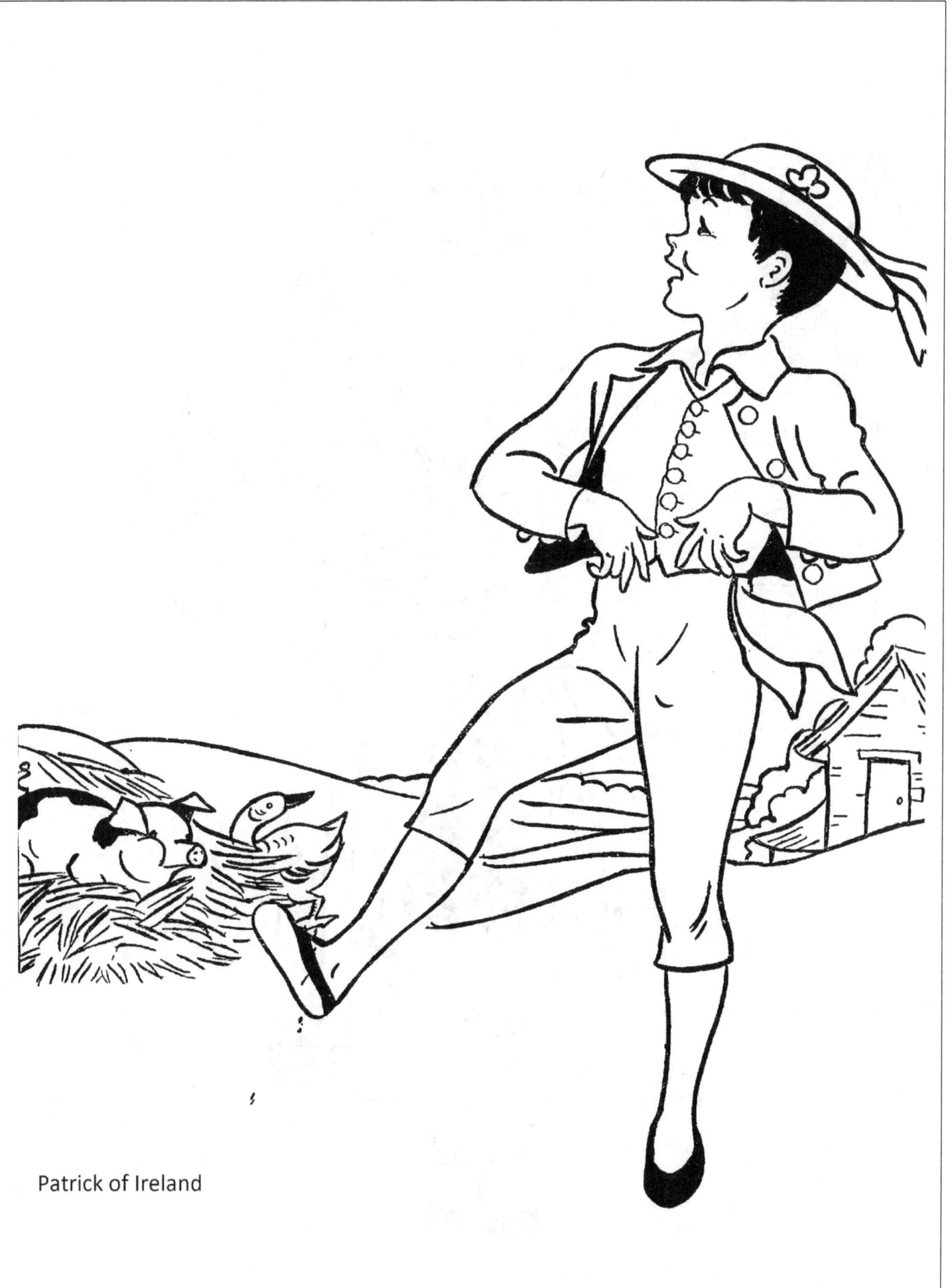

Patrick of Ireland

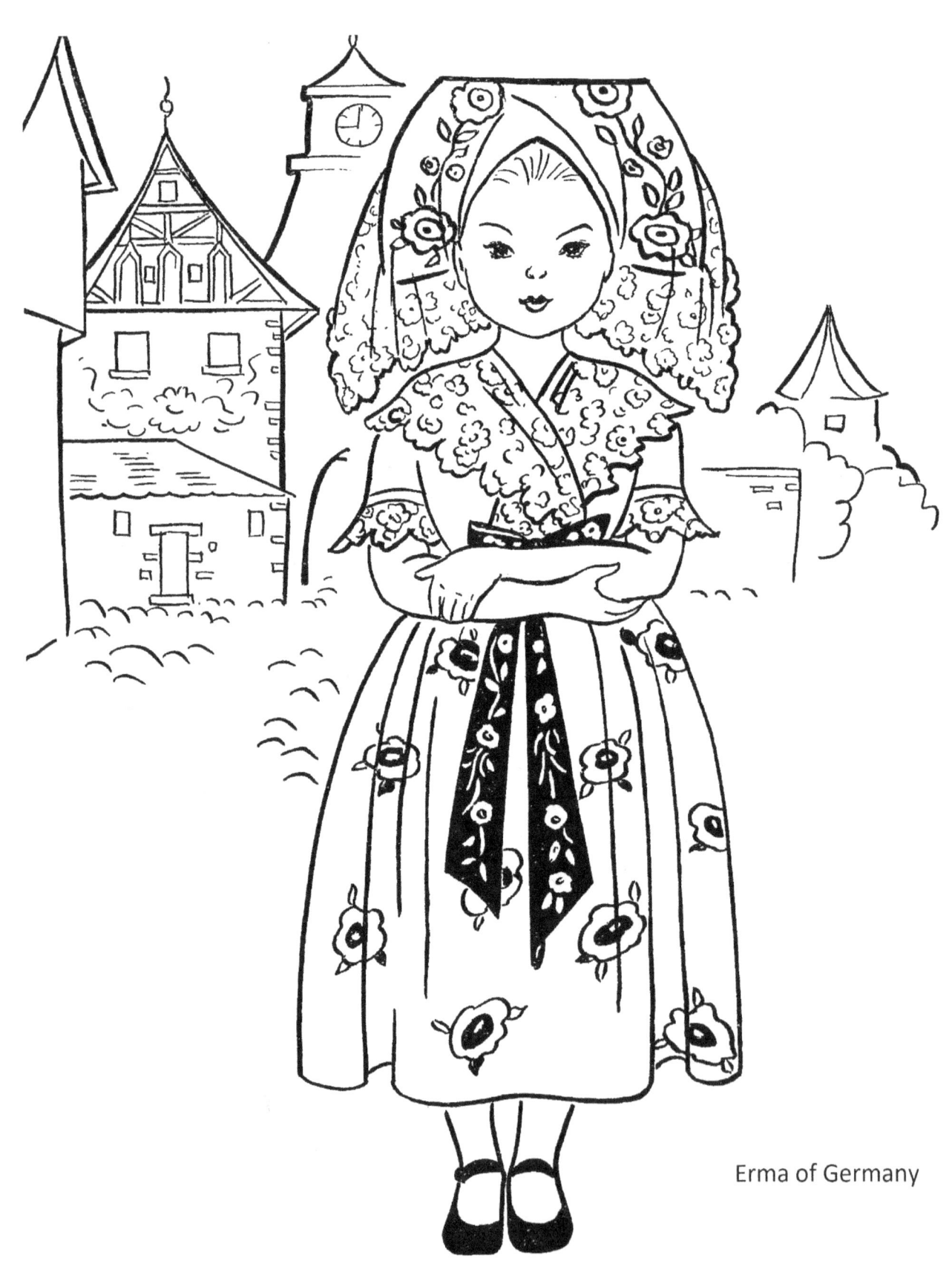

Erma of Germany

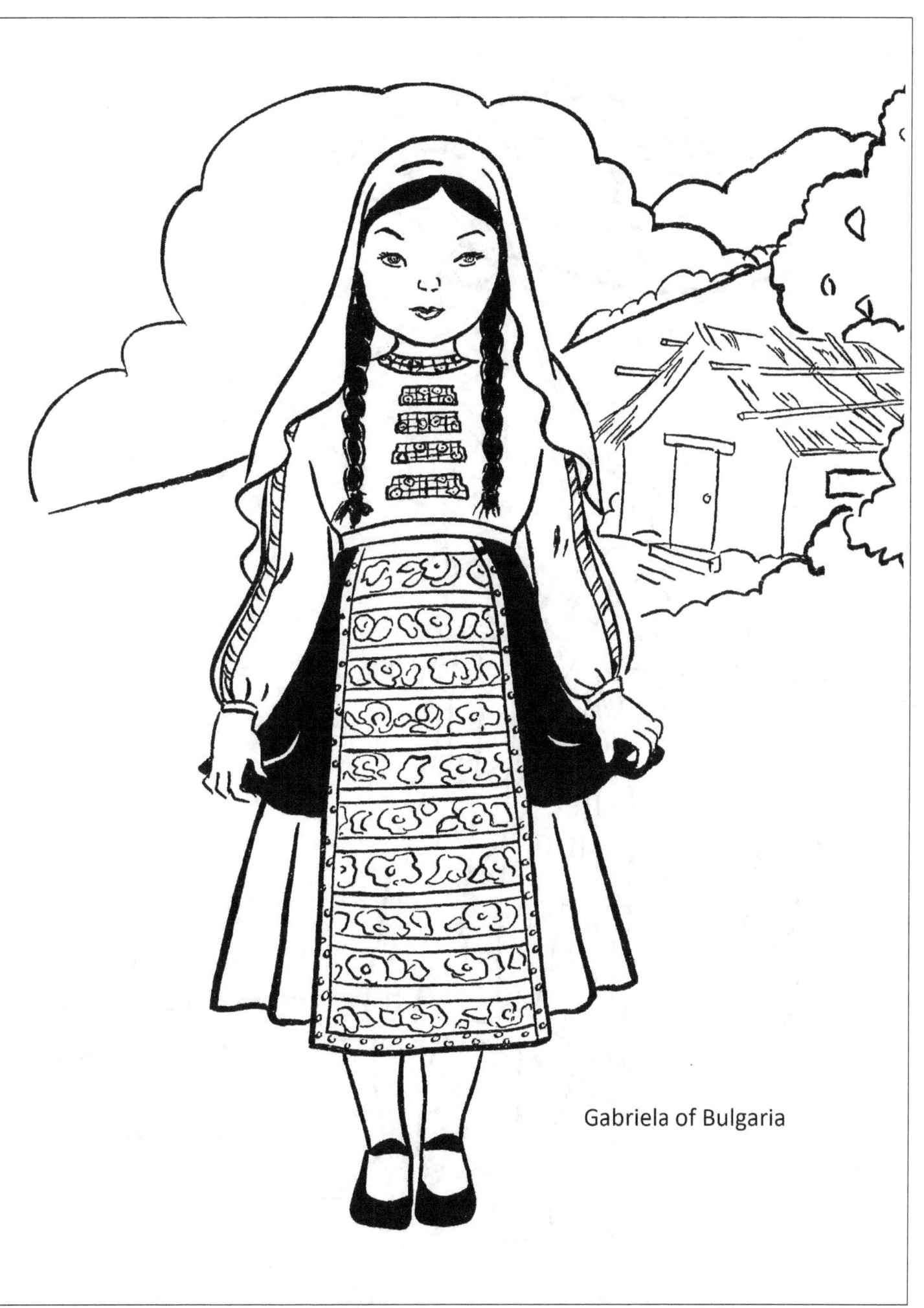

Gabriela of Bulgaria

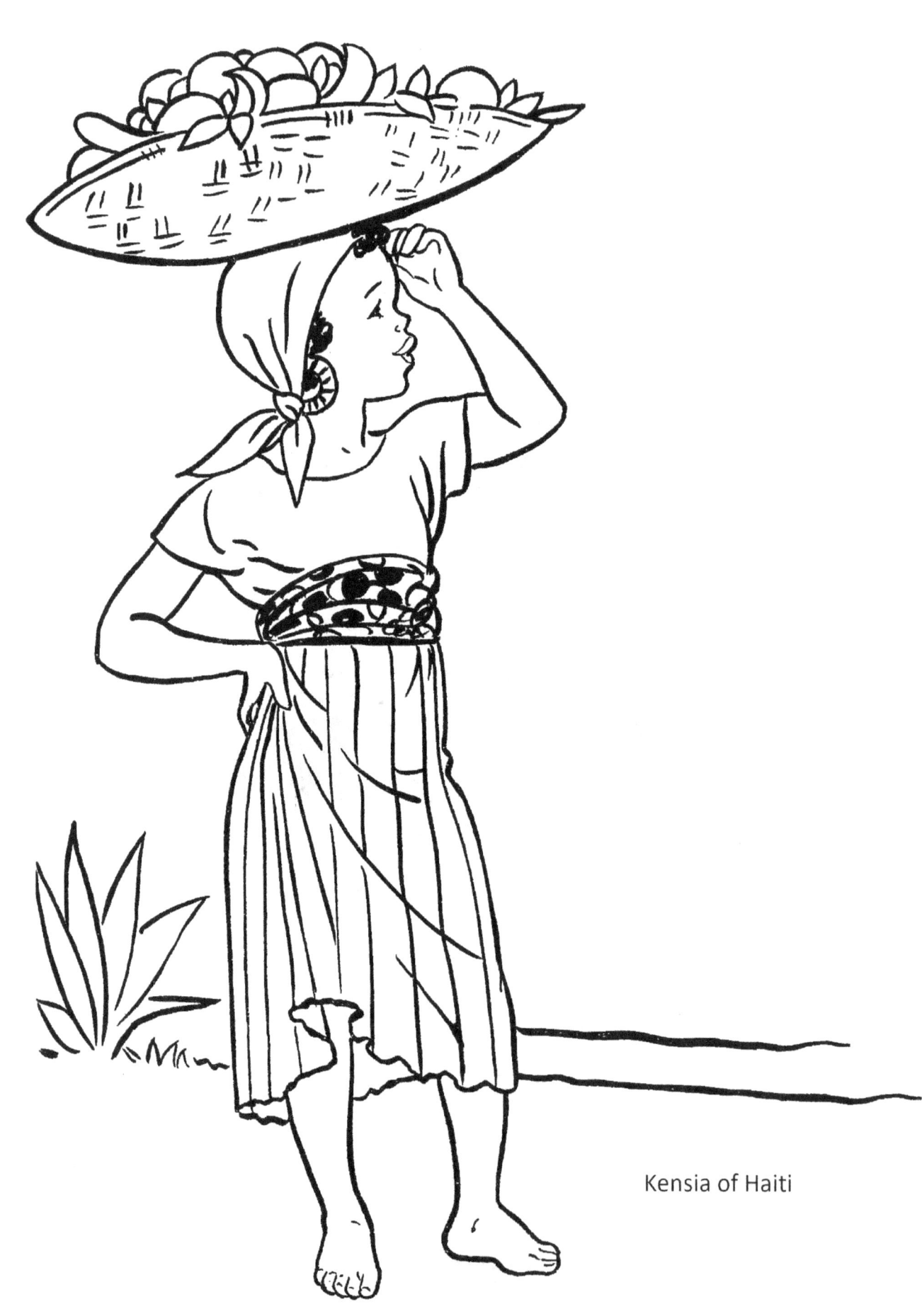

Kensia of Haiti

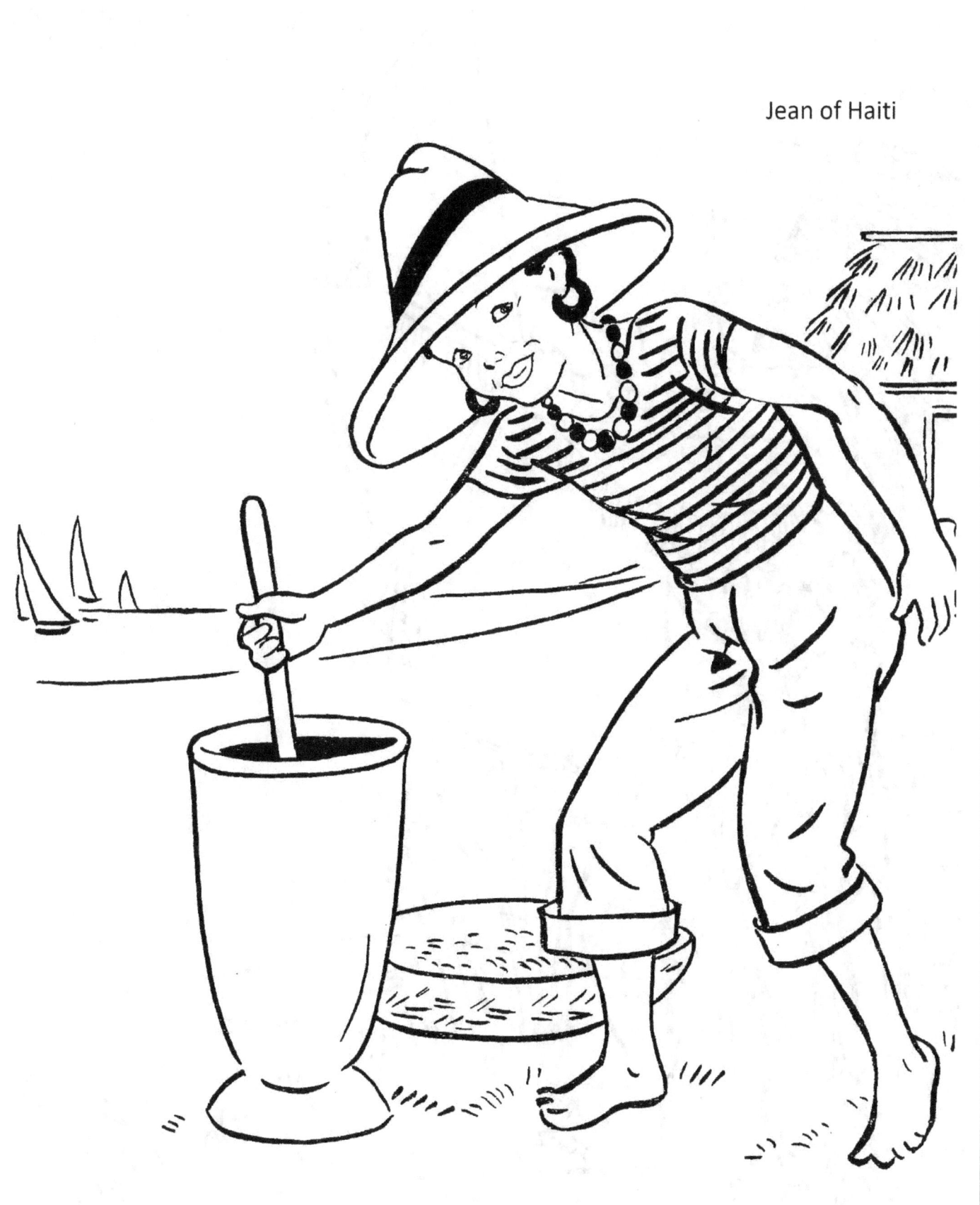

Jean of Haiti

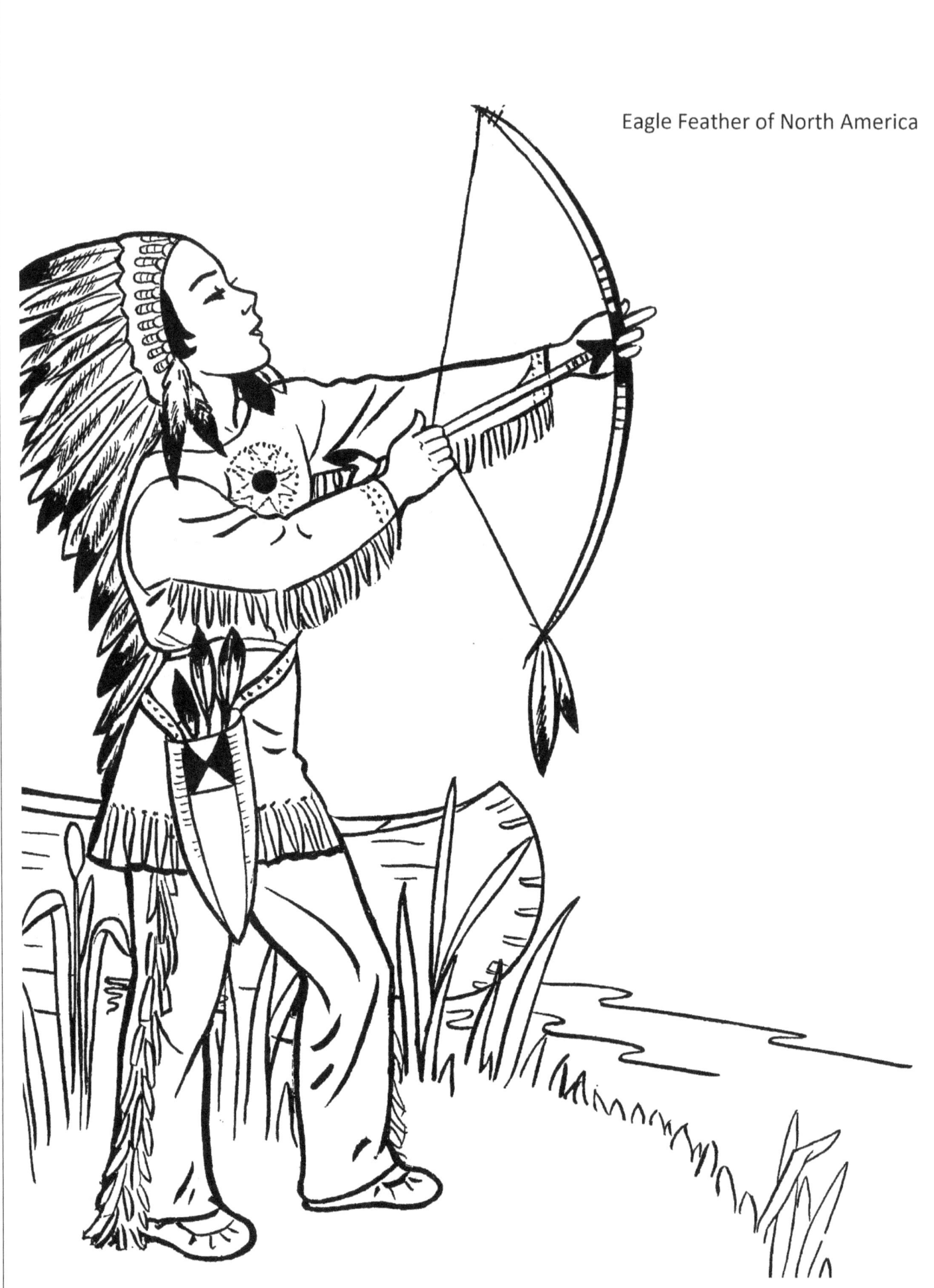

Eagle Feather of North America

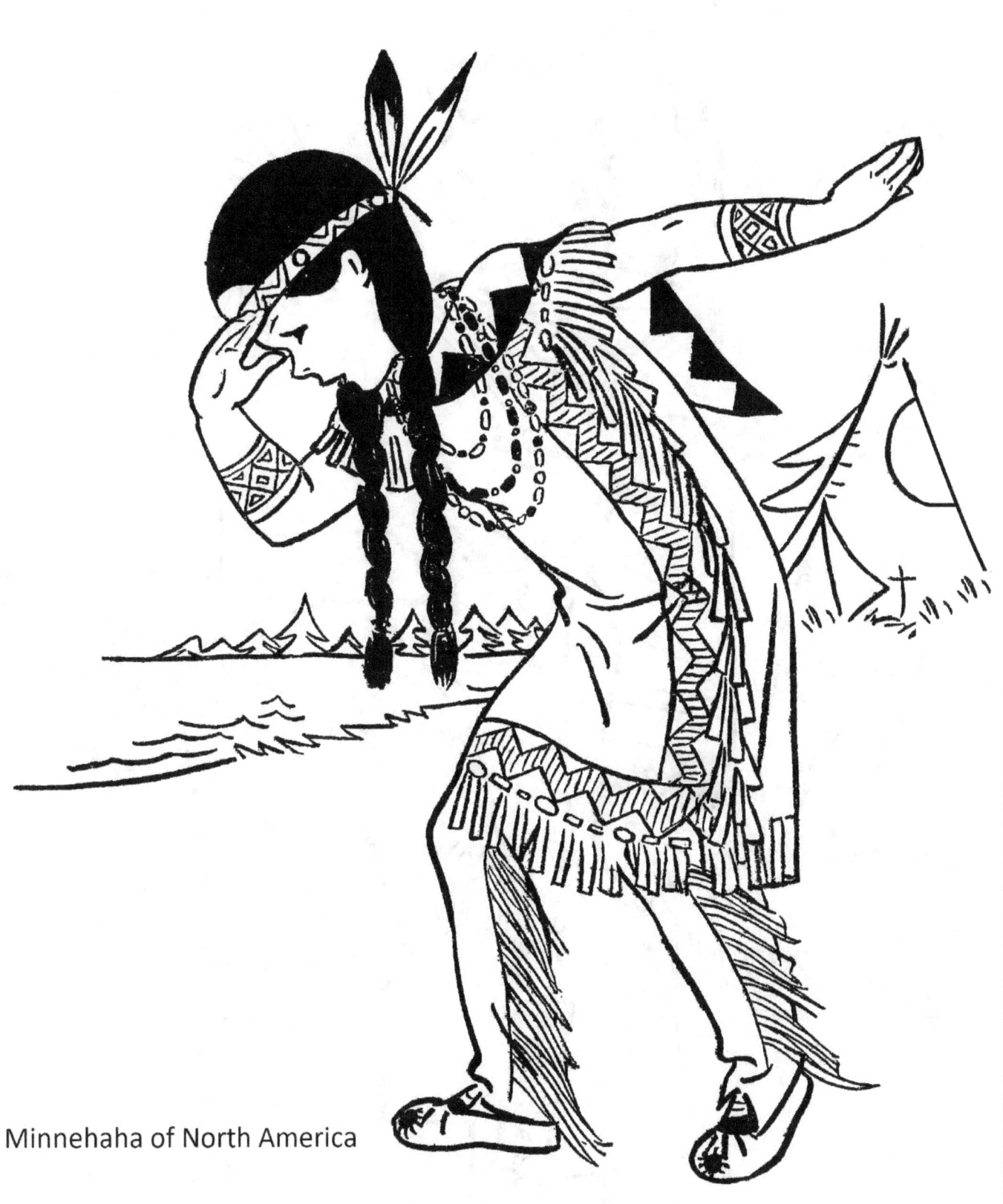

Minnehaha of North America

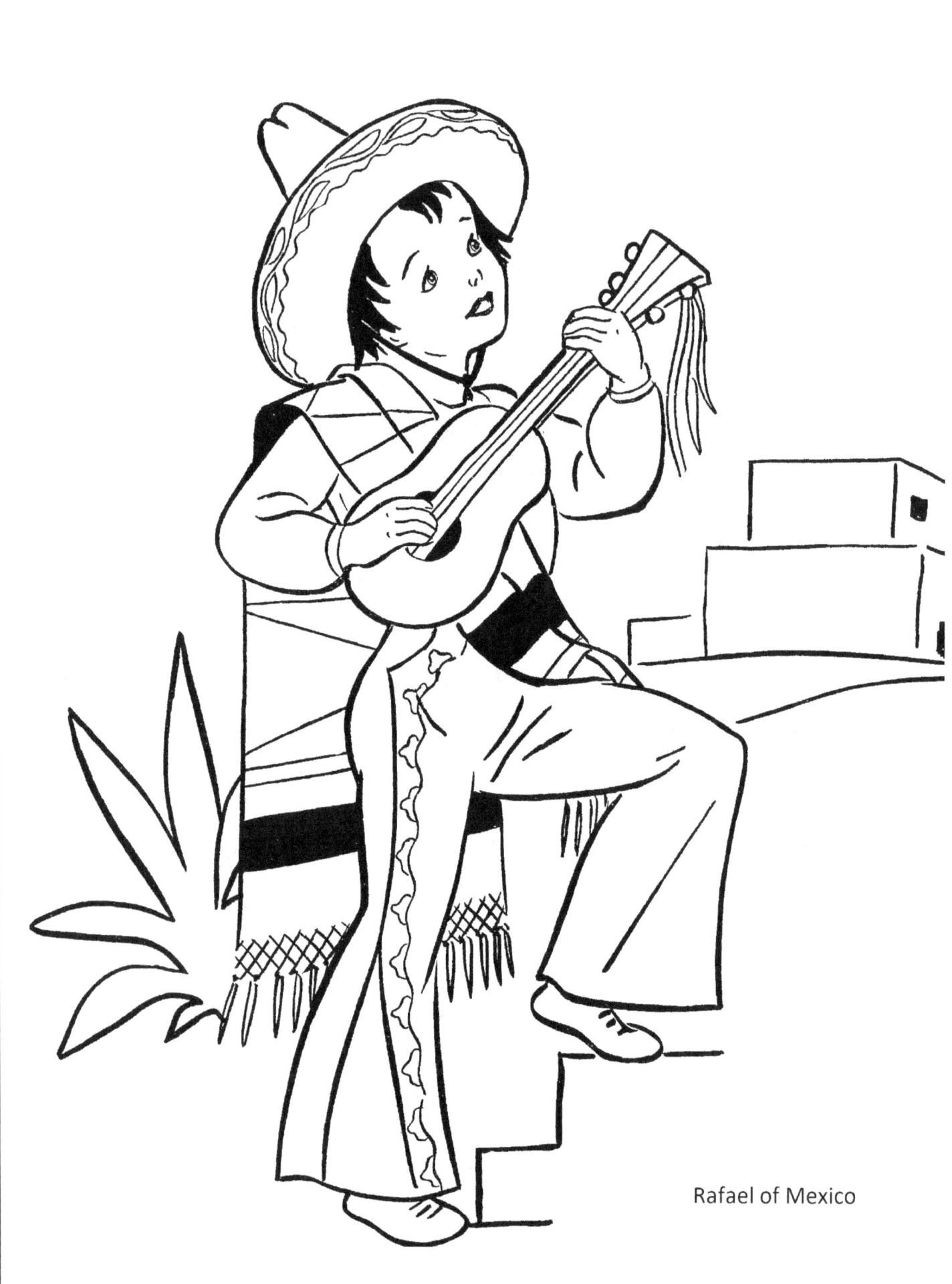

Rafael of Mexico

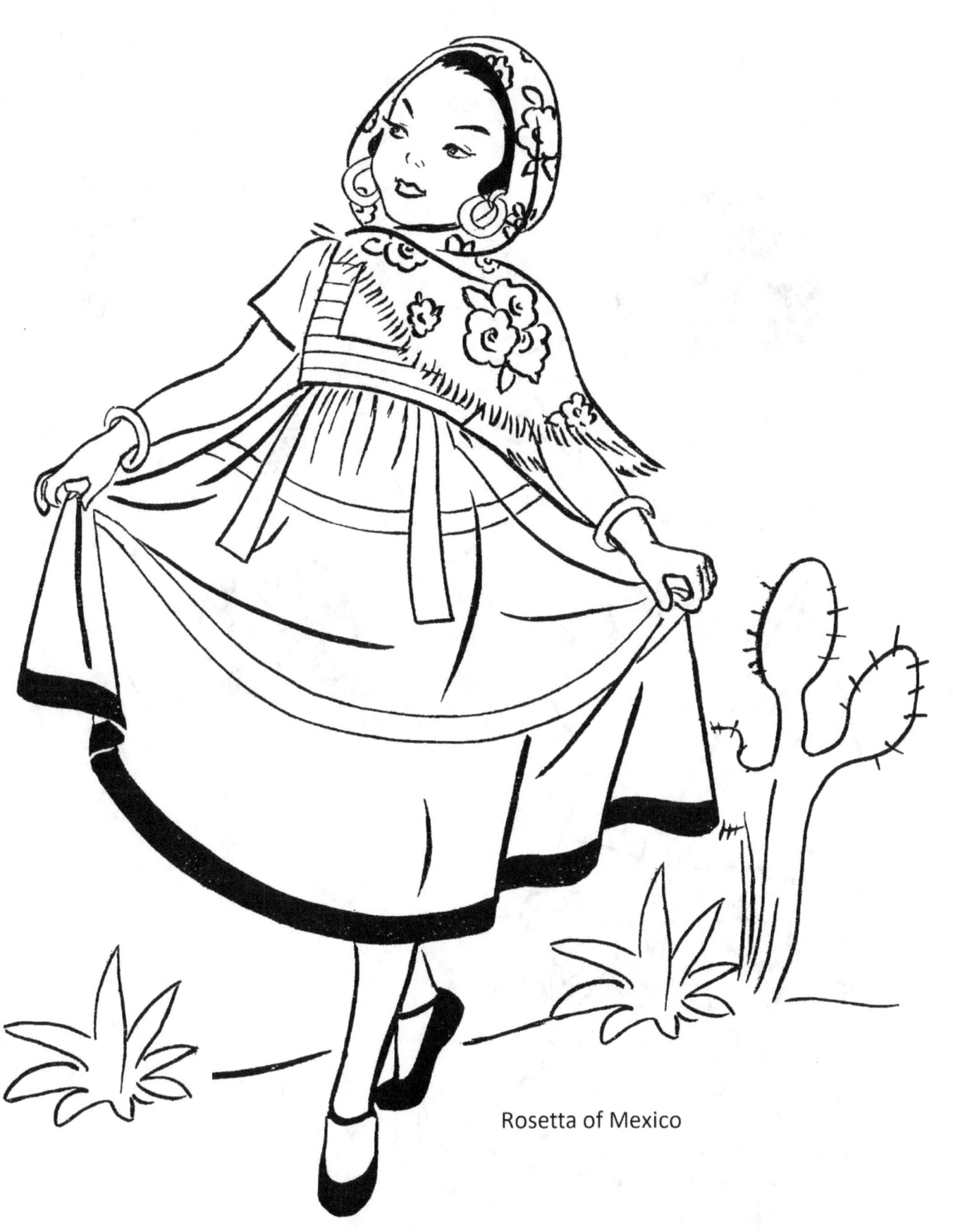

Rosetta of Mexico

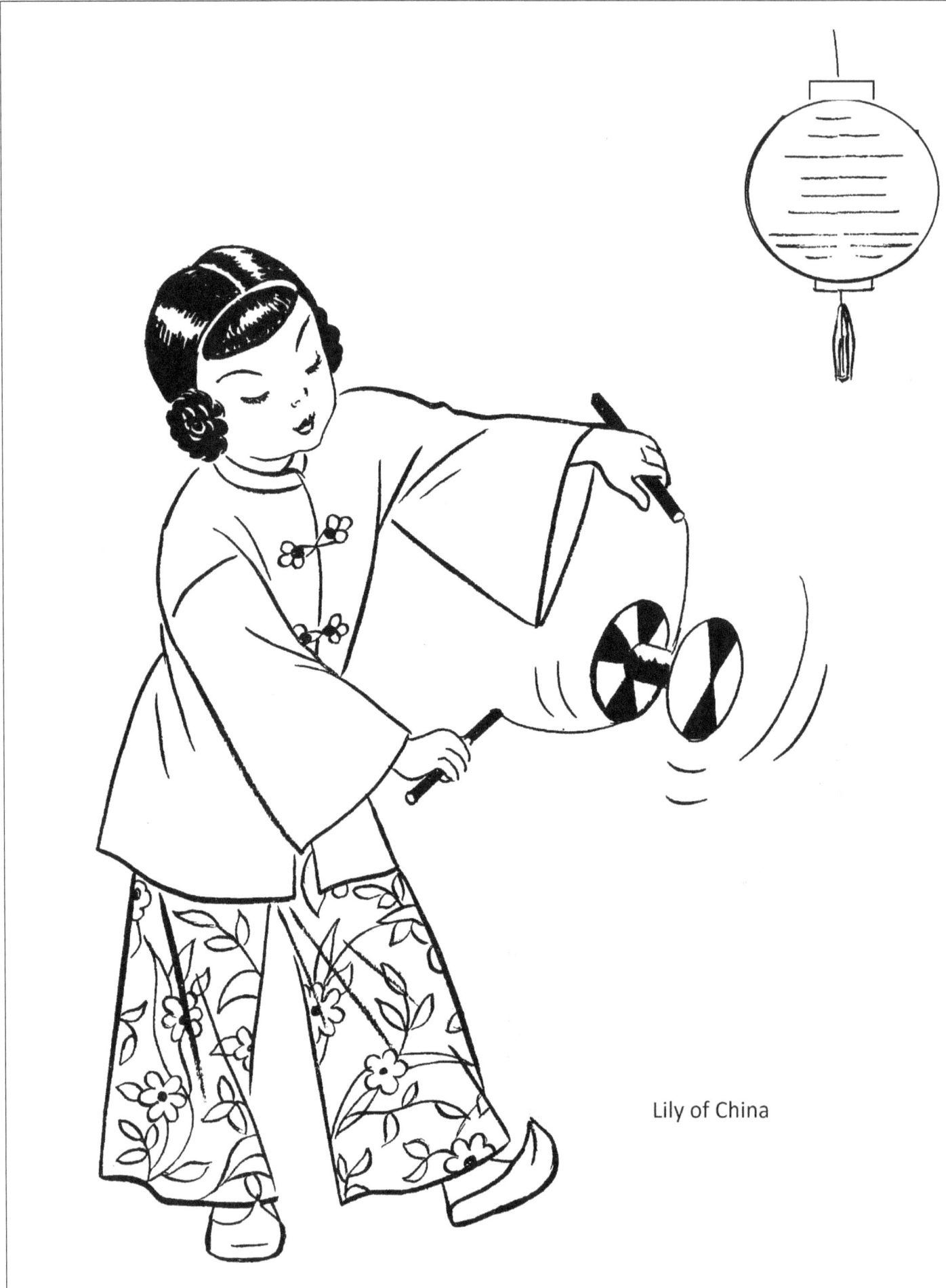

Lily of China

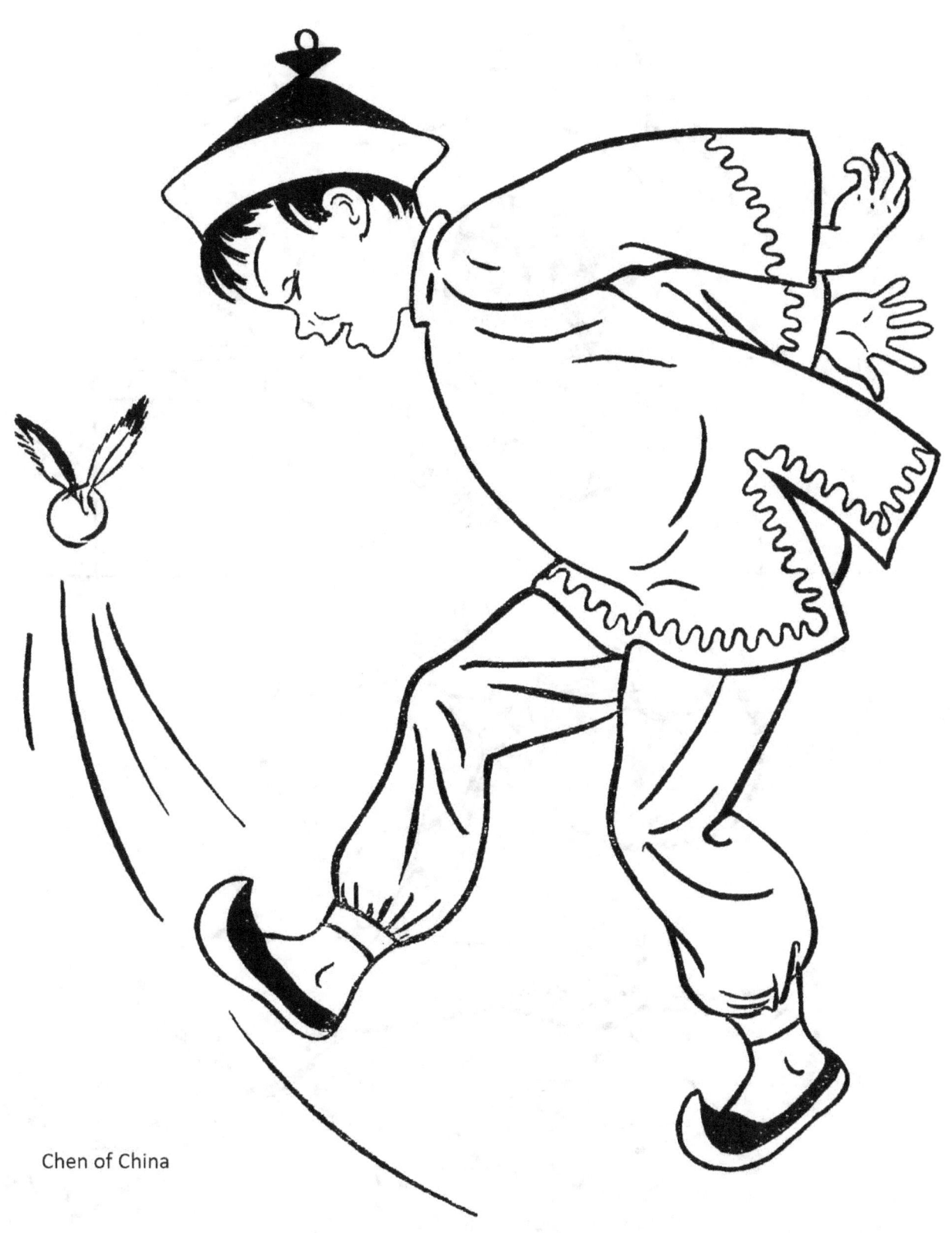

Chen of China

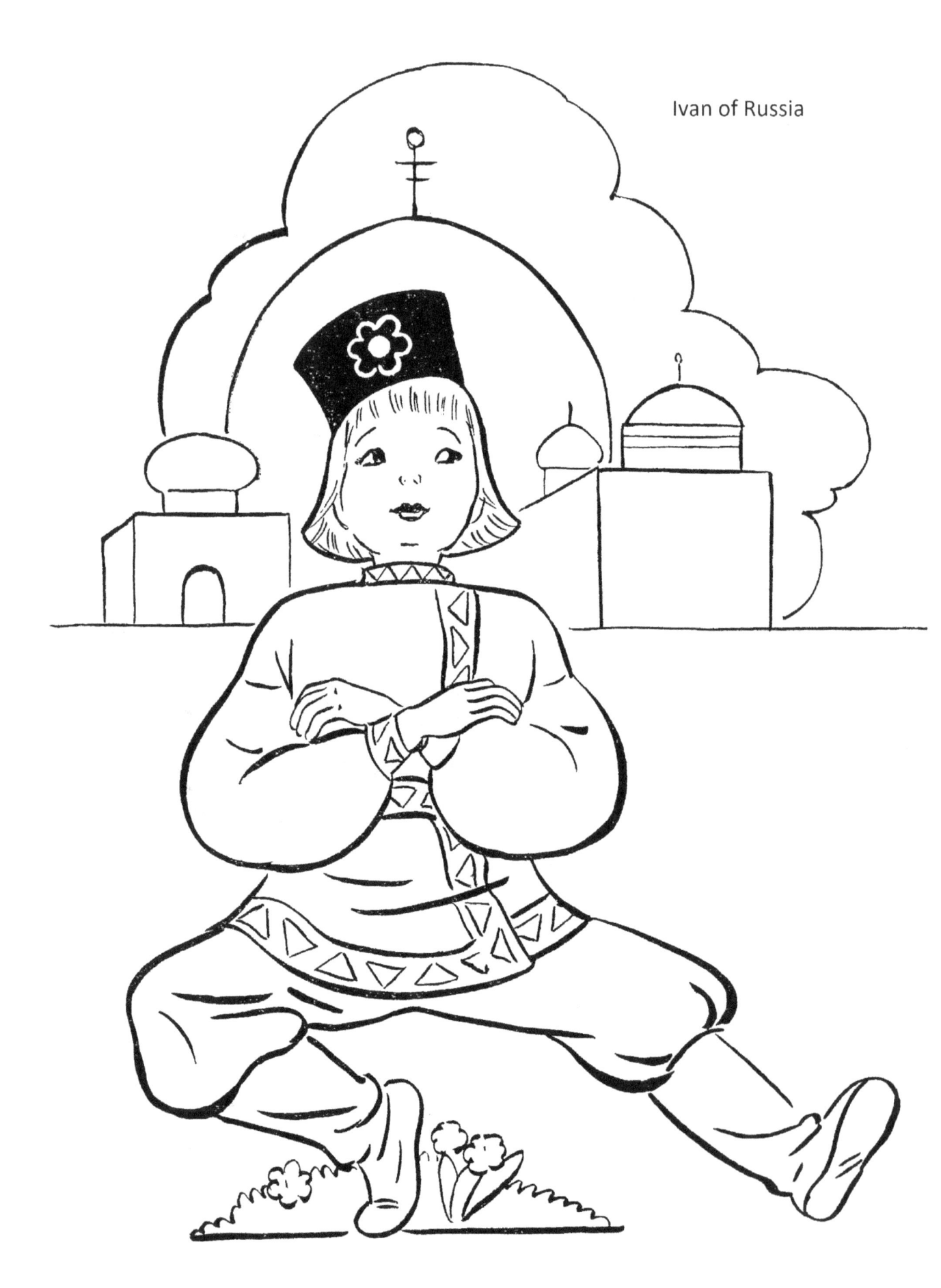

Ivan of Russia

Olga of Russia

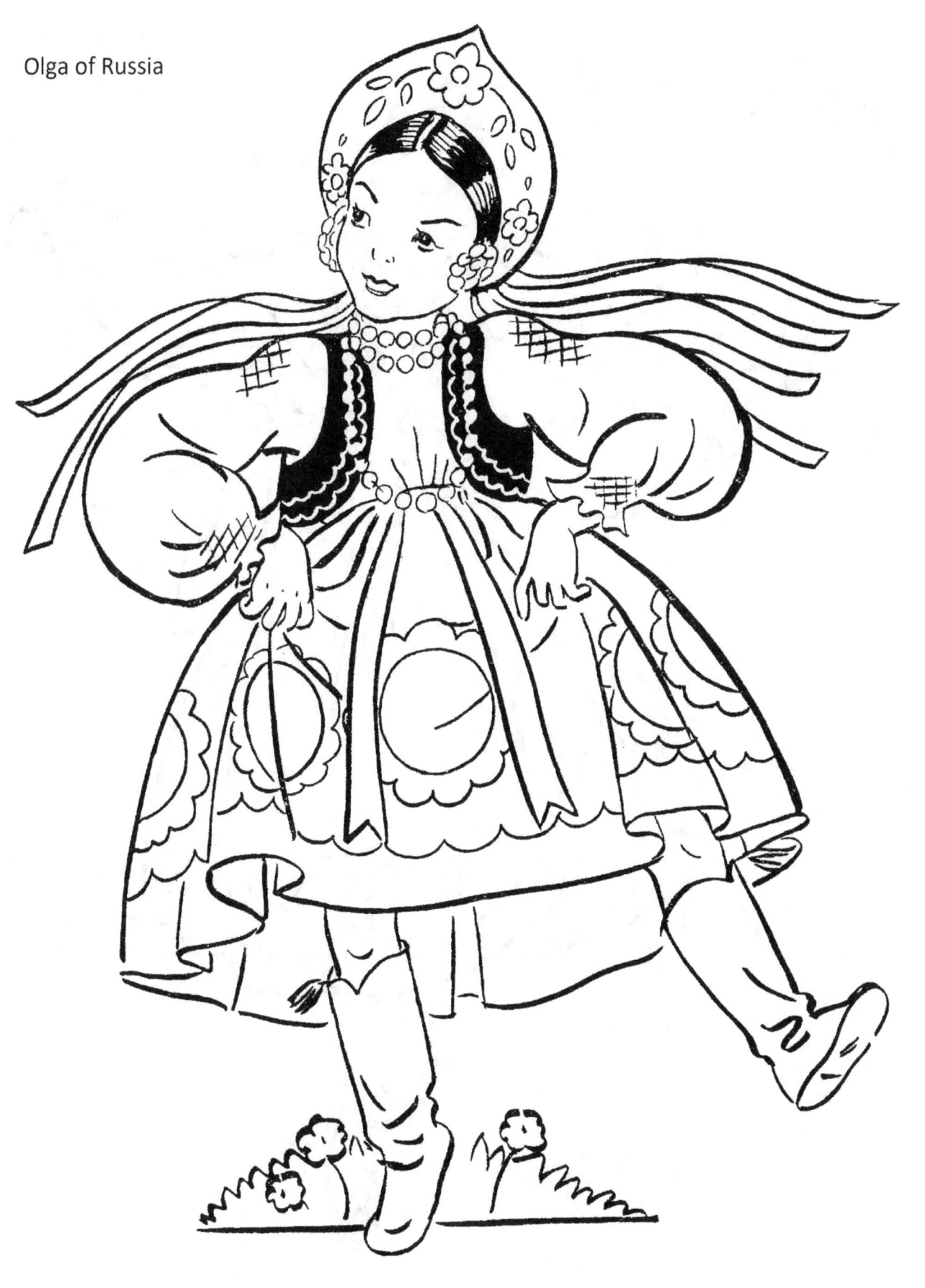

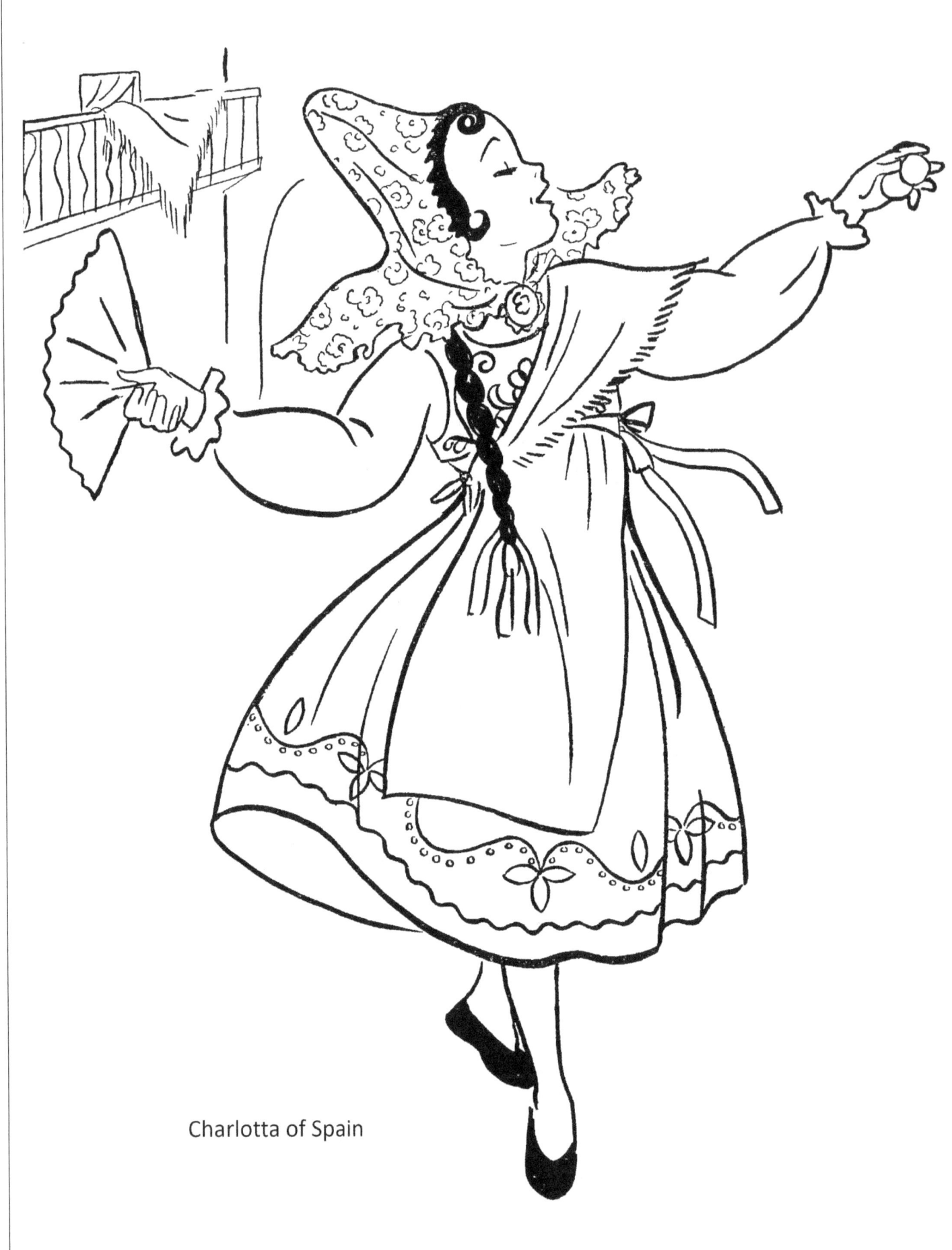

Charlotta of Spain

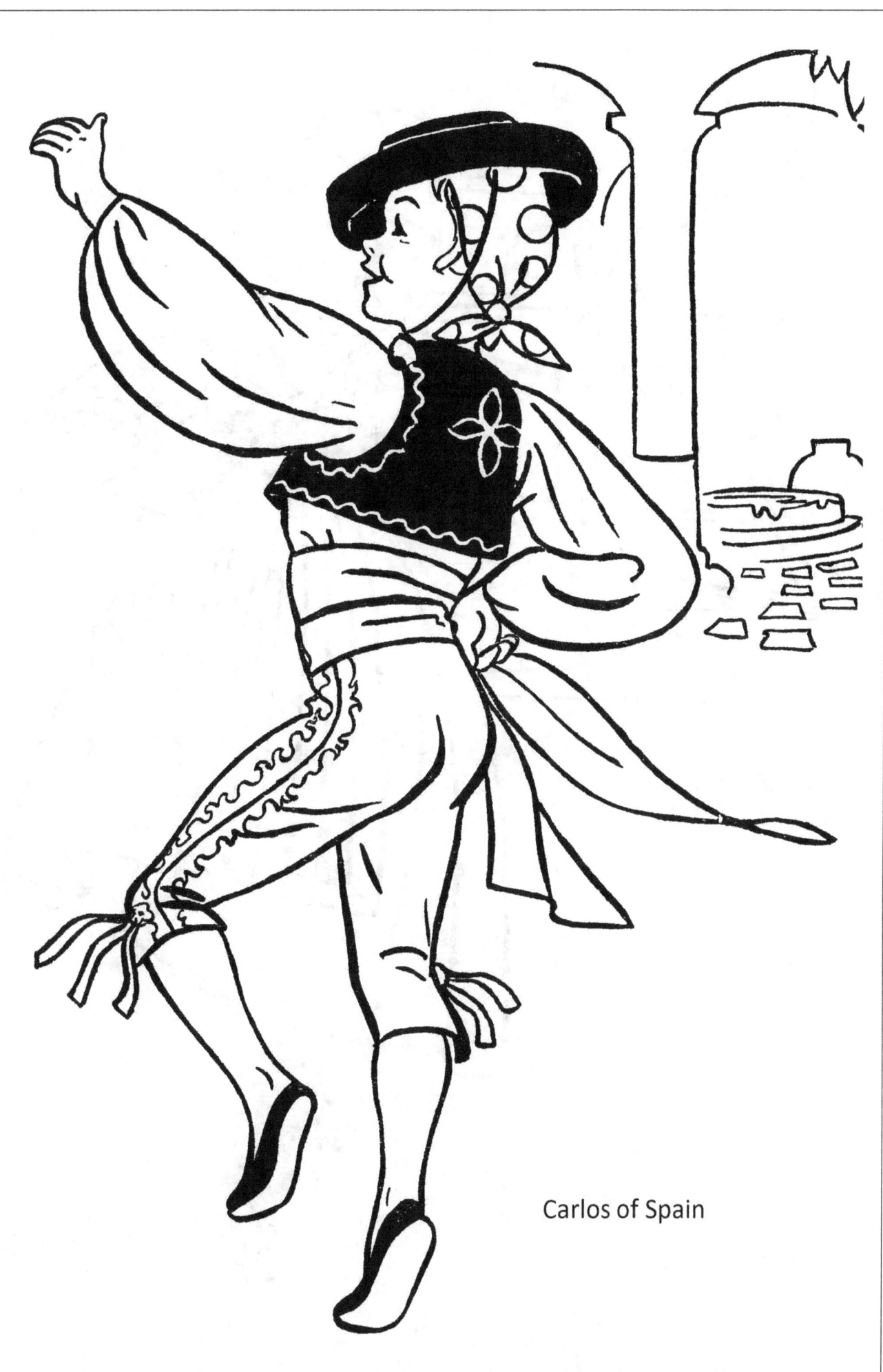

Carlos of Spain

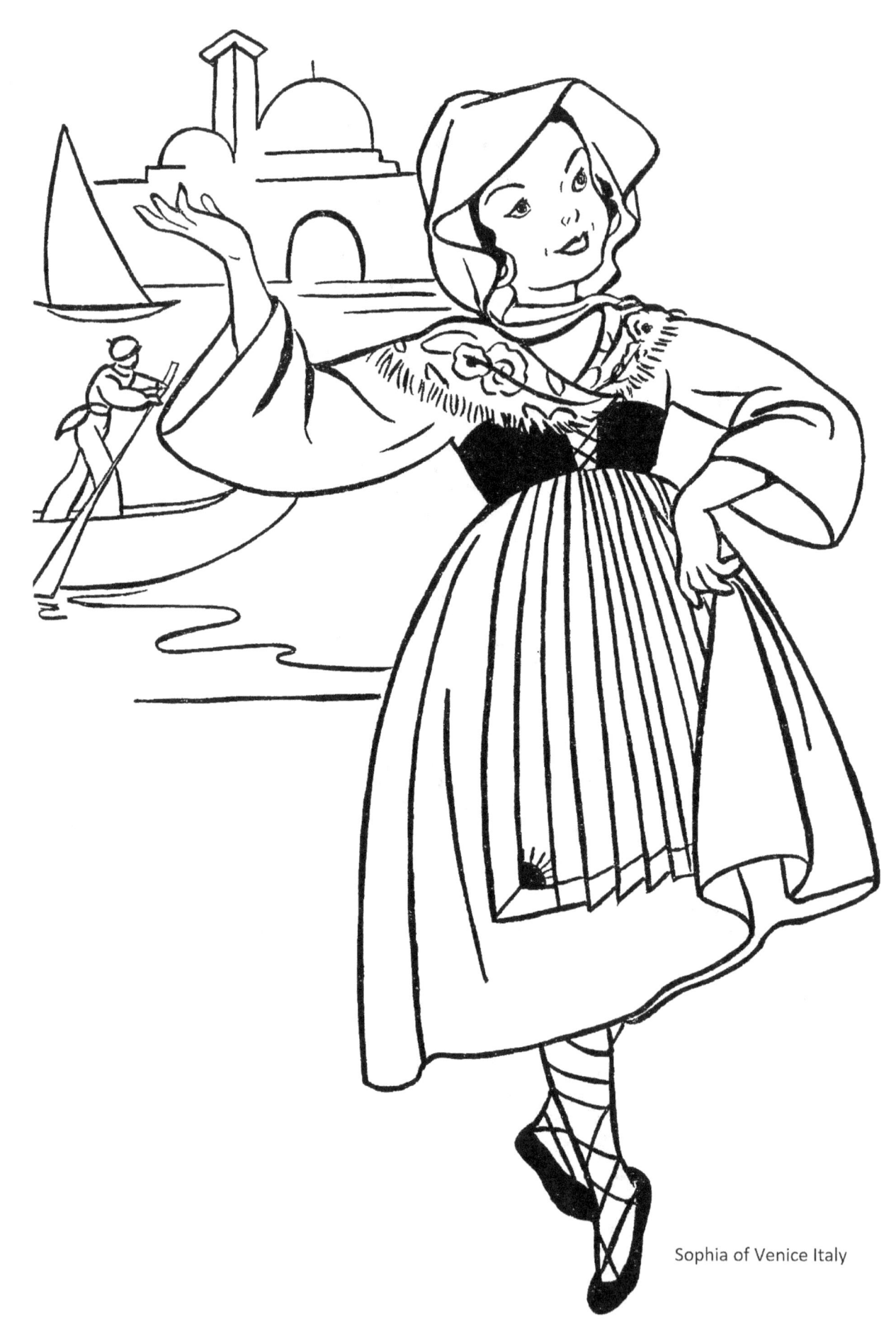

Sophia of Venice Italy

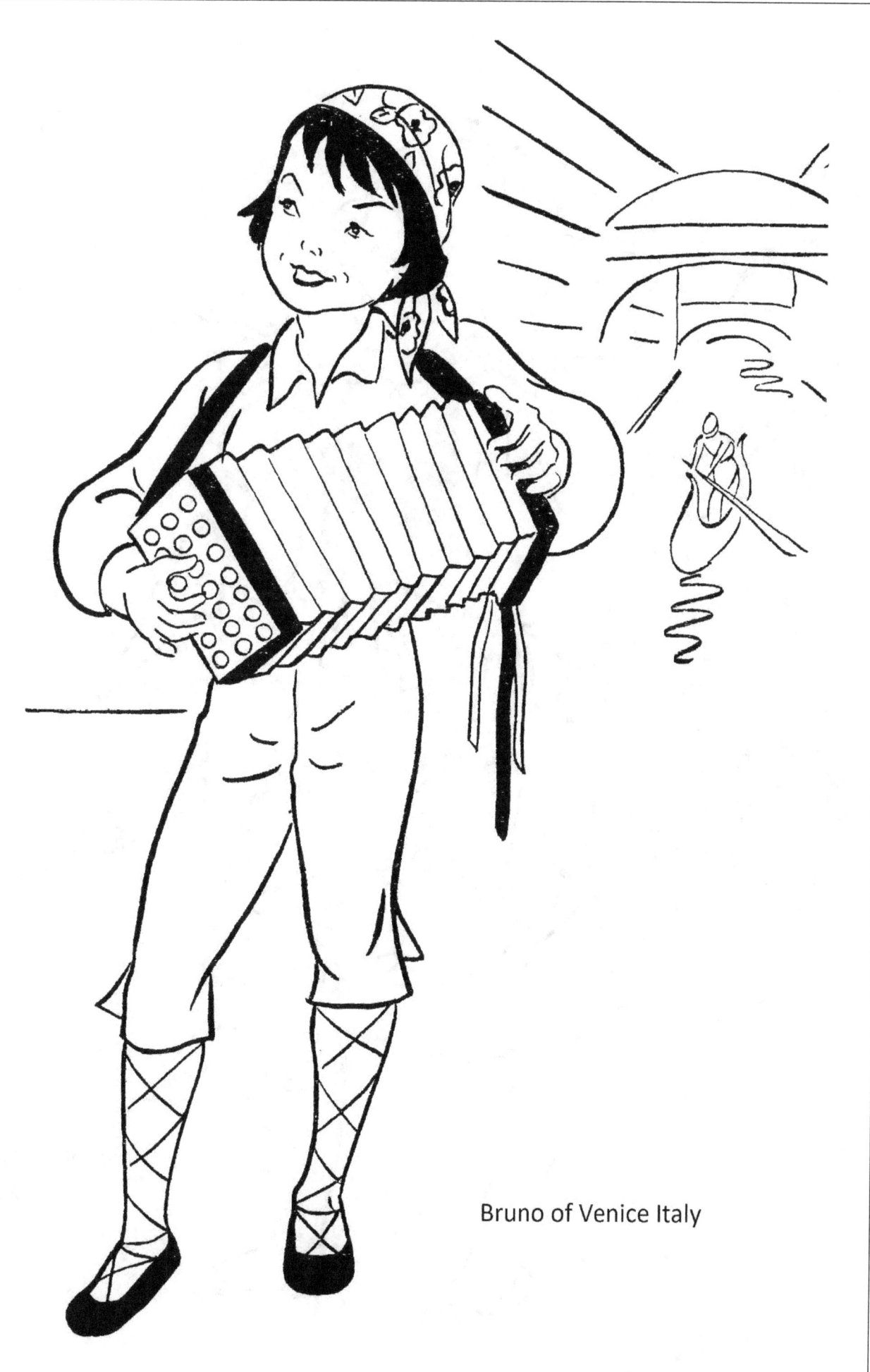

Bruno of Venice Italy

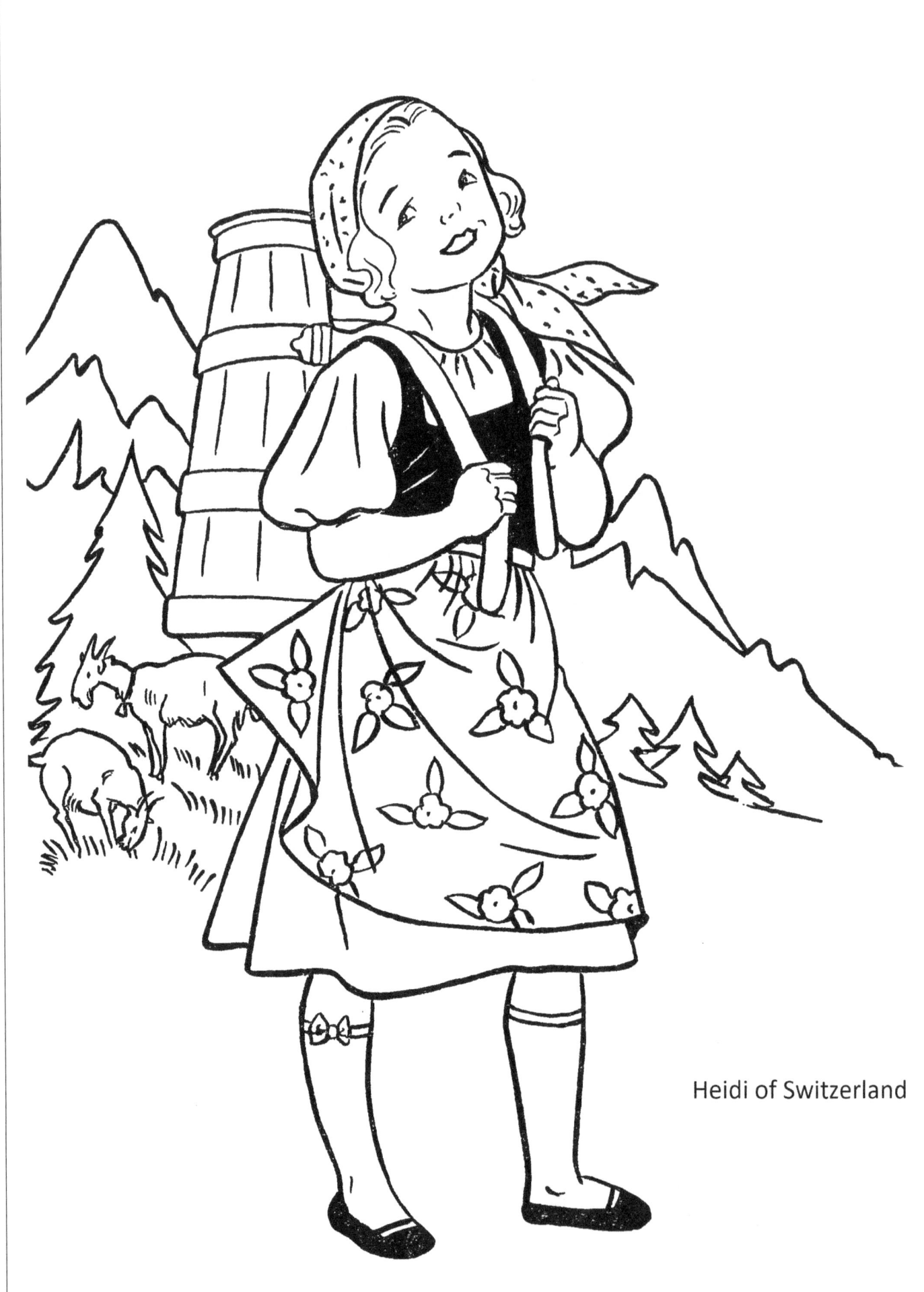

Heidi of Switzerland

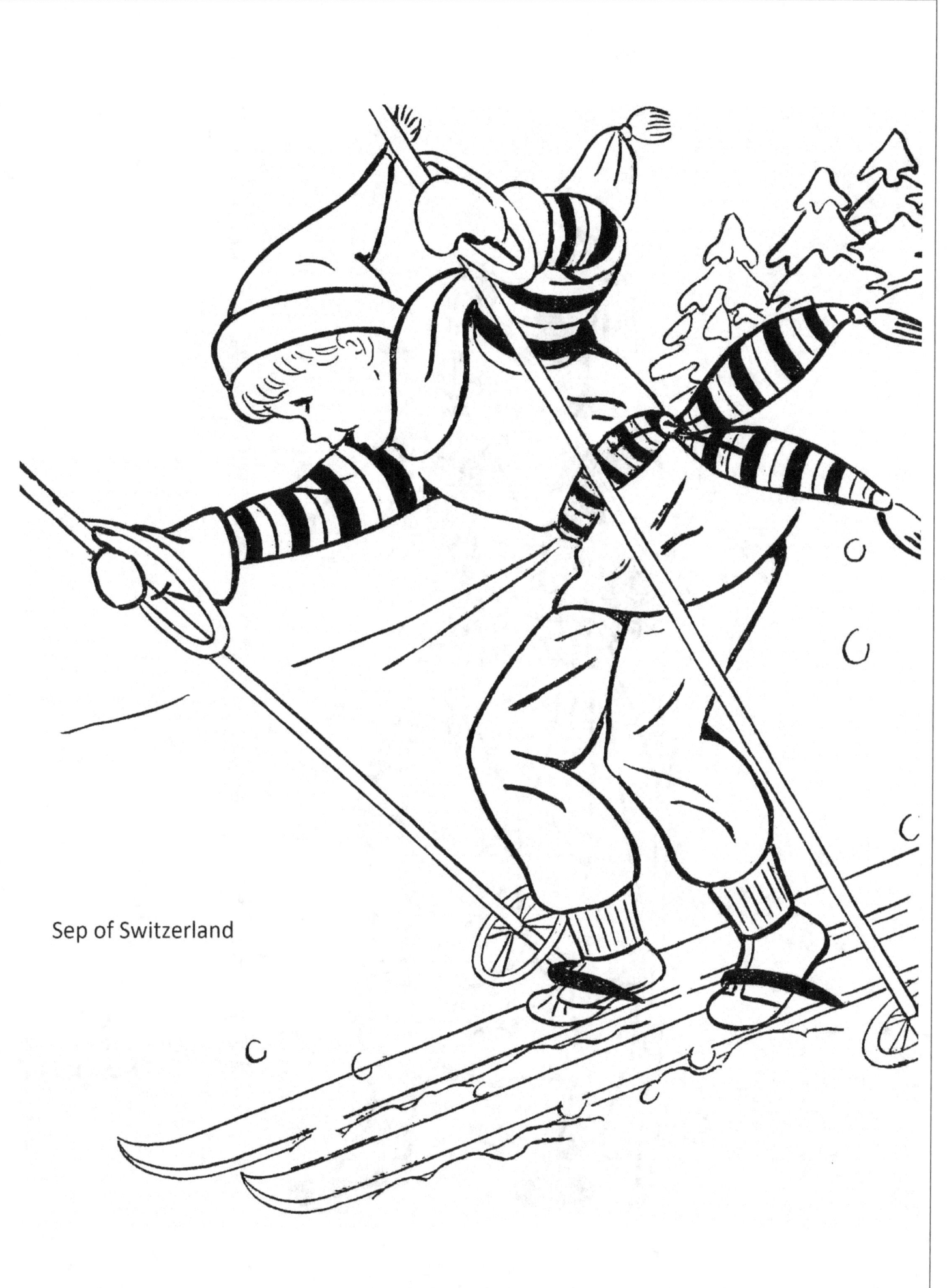

Sep of Switzerland

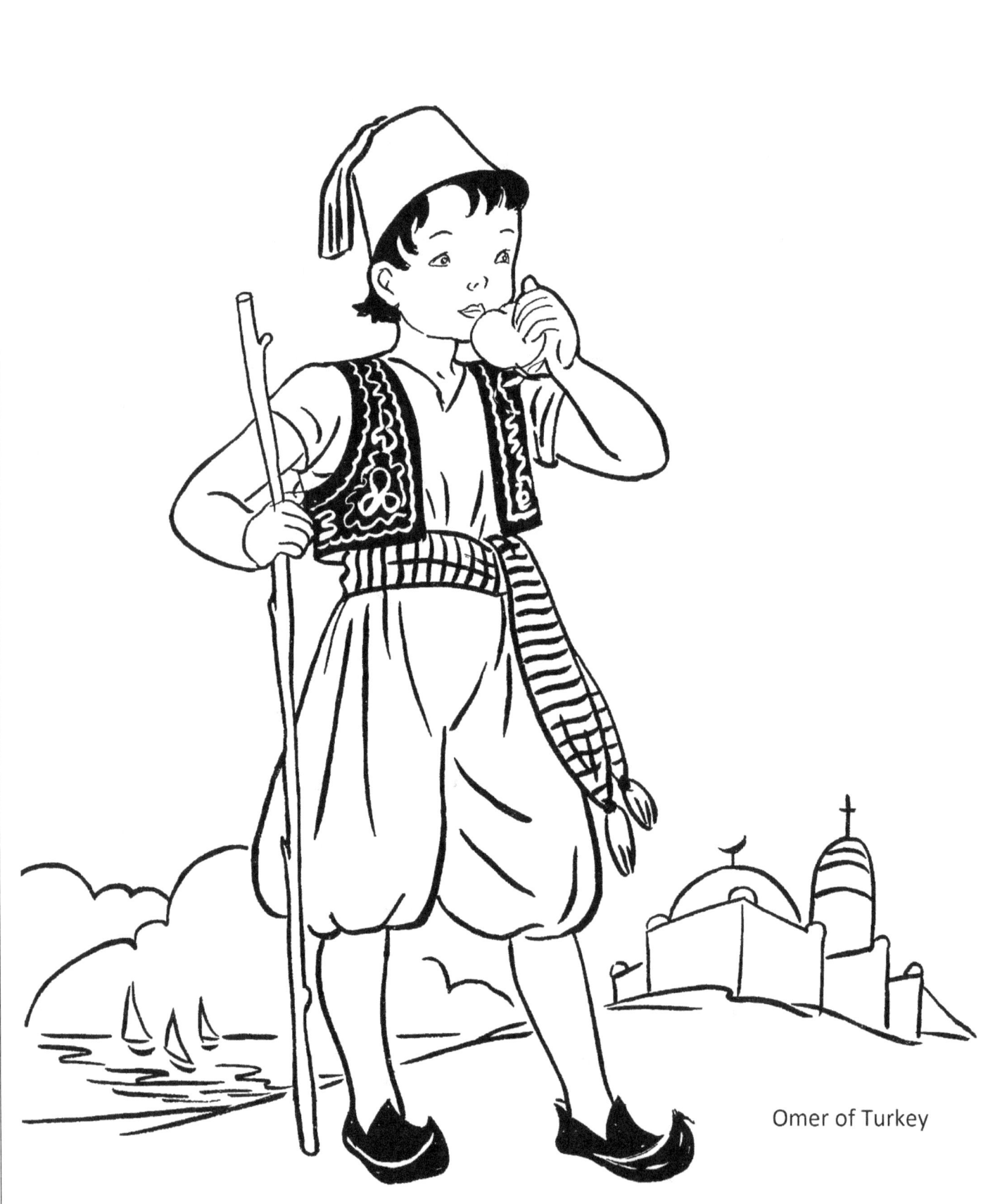

Omer of Turkey

Karl and Sari of Hungary

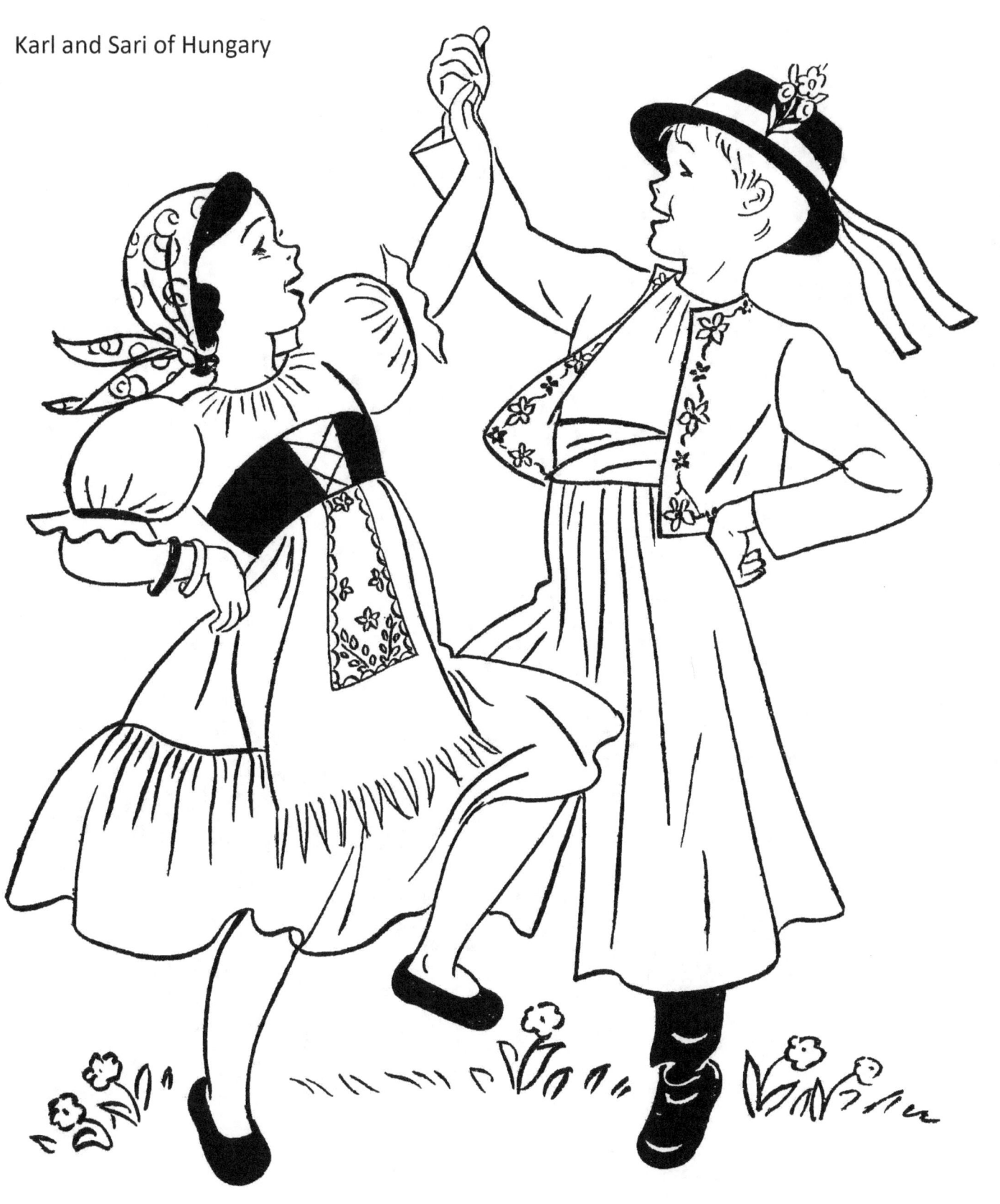